MAX GAWN
Captain's Diary

MAX GAWN

Captain's Diary

AFTER 57 YEARS: MELBOURNE'S
HISTORY-MAKING 2021 GRAND FINAL SEASON

with Konrad Marshall

Hardie Grant

BOOKS

Published in 2021 by Hardie Grant Books, an imprint of Hardie Grant Publishing

Hardie Grant Books (Melbourne)
Wurundjeri Country
Building 1, 658 Church Street
Richmond, Victoria 3121

Hardie Grant Books (London)
5th & 6th Floors
52–54 Southwark Street
London SE1 1UN

hardiegrantbooks.com

 A catalogue record for this book is available from the National Library of Australia

Max Gawn Captain's Diary
ISBN 978 1 7437 9847 8

10 9 8 7 6 5 4 3 2 1

Publisher: Pam Brewster
Cover design: Luke Causby, Blue Cork
Typeset in 12/20 pt Sabon LT Std by Kirbyjones
Cover image and all images courtesy of AFL Photos
Printed in Australia by McPhersons Printing Group.

Hardie Grant acknowledges the Traditional Owners of the country on which we work, the Wurundjeri people of the Kulin nation and the Gadigal people of the Eora nation, and recognises their continuing connection to the land, waters and culture. We pay our respects to their Elders past, present and emerging.

To all Melbourne fans, we did it, after 57 years we brought it home!

CONTENTS

CHAPTER 1
Post-season, Pre-season

People always ask me what changed at Melbourne. When did you turn the corner? What decision made the difference? Which person played the biggest part? I get that. As a lover of the game and of my club, I completely understand that curiosity. It's human nature. We need that sense of meaning, don't we, particularly here in this amazing, joyful moment as AFL premiers. We're a good story, the Demons, and good stories rely on understanding 'the moment that changed everything'.

But of course there's no one answer. There are a thousand answers. I like to think that what we've achieved this season at the Melbourne Football Club – a 13th flag, 57 years after our 12th – is the outcome of a slow burn from 2015. Do you remember 2015? I do and I don't. It feels like an eternity ago.

Paul Roos was our coach. Nathan Jones was our captain. So far, so familiar. But do you remember who was vice captain? Lynden Dunn was our deputy. Can you remember the exact make-up of the leadership group? I had to look it up to get it right: Daniel Cross, Chris Dawes, Jack Grimes and Heretier Lumumba. Jesse Hogan won the AFL Rising Star. Bernie Vince won the Keith 'Bluey' Truscott Medal as our team's best and fairest. We finished in 13th spot.

Yeah. Six years in the past. An eternity ago.

I could trace every slip and jump since then, in detail. I could think through every rise and every fall, but it would take too long here. And yet there's definitely one small moment I want to dwell on, because it was a turning point in my growth, and I wonder sometimes if that kind of moment is what some of my teammates have gone through in these past 18 months, as things between us have gotten more honest and open and true.

Basically, I was young, and finding my feet. In 2013 and 2014 I was playing one game in the VFL, one in the AFL, in and out and just unable to take those opportunities. If you haven't enjoyed the thrill of playing AFL as an established senior – if you're still emerging and grasping for your spot in the best 22 – then 'oldest player in the VFL team' is not a title you want, but that was me in 2015. I was 24, and not quite sinking, but certainly treading water. The feedback I got from Paul Roos was in my face, and direct: 'Pull your head out of your arse.' I remember we played a game against Fremantle in Darwin, and Garrick Ibbotson bodied me out in a marking contest. He was a great player, but he was also 186 centimetres and maybe 80 kilograms sopping wet. I was bigger, and stronger, and should have done better. I got subbed out immediately. Again, Roosy was direct with me, and in front of the group, too: 'You muscle people out all day in the VFL ... and then come out here and do *nothing!*' The little point I'm making here is not about the value of a coach firing up and delivering a spray. Nor is it a message about needing thick skin to survive in this game. The idea is that criticism can come from a good place, and when it does – when it's pure and correct and deserved and real – it makes all the difference.

That's why it's worth starting this book closer to the present, but farther from home – in Queensland in 2020, when we were stuck in the hub in Twin Waters on the Sunshine Coast, in the back half of a pandemic-affected season. It sounds claustrophobic, doesn't it, hublife? Locked down. Locked in. Tucked away from the world, surrounded by the same people day and night, night and day. But I look back now and it seems a key factor in the way we shifted. Daily, hourly contact meant daily, hourly conversations.

What was good about the hub? Being around families, for one. We talk always about being a family club – most clubs do. But we were finally creating that environment in a tangible way. It wasn't just something we wrote in mission statements on our website. As AFL players, you naturally meet some of your coaches' partners and families, but we suddenly got to see so many of these people up close, at breakfast, lunch and dinner. Jake Lever and Jack Viney both had kids who were no older than six weeks, so I was part of Daddy Day Care. Nathan Jones and Neville Jetta – their families were bloody everywhere. When we were giving our votes for 'best on' in the hub, Teddy Melksham – Jake Melksham's middle son – almost got the three votes.

And that sense of family spread even more widely. We began connecting more deeply with past players, even though they couldn't be there. I remember hearing from David Neitz, and him talking to us through a screen, telling us how much football meant to him in isolation, how much watching the Demons while being locked down in Melbourne was doing for everyone back home.

When you're living your entire life in communal dining spaces, and retreating 'home' to a room in a resort, everything seems outsized. Bigger. Louder. More vivid. More important. Hublife magnifies everything – the good and the bad – and for us that meant two things. First, we were playing good football at the tail end of 2020, going 8 and 5 while living together in the tropics. That's the great part – feeling the team mingle and coalesce and come together on field. The second part was both bad and good. And it was cultural.

There was something about the way we were talking to one another, socially as much as professionally. It was too casual, or dismissive perhaps. We were having a laugh at one another's expense, and doing it too often. It would be easy to say it was the laid-back Sunshine Coast seeping into our daily lives, but we began to see things that might sound minor or petty – *perhaps not worthy of attention and analysis* – yet I wasn't so sure. It felt like something we shouldn't take into 2021.

I'll give you an example. Multiple times – to get a cheap laugh – someone would say, 'Yeah, Jake Lever had a great game – but he doesn't play on anyone.' That's something you hear outside the club – that Jake takes intercept marks all day because he's not responsible for an opponent. Now, it's not true. Jake Lever *does* play on someone. He *always* plays on someone. He's just really good at reading the ball and making good decisions and knowing when to leave his man. But we would make that joke anyway. I've made that joke myself. And that joke would bring Jake Lever down. These are things that had been going on for years, and they needed to stop. It wouldn't require a massive change – just a renewed awareness, and an effort to scrap them, stripping those things out, to make people feel better about themselves, not worse. We found something bad and turned it into something good.

There's one other thing that happened in the hub. We went to Cairns, and it was horrible. We lost twice, to two sides we should have beaten, in Round 15 against Sydney and Round 16 against the Dockers, and we dropped outside of the eight. These were teams below us, and those losses were almost an aberration compared to our other form, but that doesn't matter. In those five days – the games were on a Thursday and the following Monday – we had cost ourselves a place in the finals. And that spurred so many conversations. Almost too many conversations. Crisis meetings, really, trying to split too many atoms. Talk and more talk became a catalyst for even more talk, for our leaders to gather and make a pledge for change. Every team makes those kinds of statements, of course, but there was something about that connection in the hub, combined with the great footy we had played, and the sting of those defeats in Cairns, that made everyone seem more clear-headed about what we needed to do in the off-season. We knew we had to attack it with aggression.

For me, that meant running, cycling, and gym sessions. I live down on the Mornington Peninsula, and trained often with Adam Tomlinson. Just the two of us running in the heat with our dogs. It's actually more fun than it sounds. I was drafted in 2009 and have been in the system a dozen years now, and there's something about the off-season that you don't want to waste. It's not exactly freedom, but freedom from surveillance. It's that one extended chance you get to run without your uniform on, without a GPS tracker slipped into the pocket at the top of your guernsey, without a prescribed group, or time, or duration. We found a deserted oval. Dogs off lead. Shackles off players.

People assume we hate training because we do it so much, especially the way it creeps into every part of your life, demanding your attention. And that can be true. But it's equally true that we *love* training. We just don't love always being monitored, always in kit, always on time. Running hard alone, and keeping yourself in check – that frees up your mind. And there really was something going on in our minds. Little things all throughout that break made that clear.

There was a low-key review of the football department, or rather, a review *for* the football department. Our CEO, Gary Pert, had conducted 42 interviews with players and coaches, benchmarking our operation against everyone from Port Adelaide to the Melbourne Storm. He came to see what most of us already knew: we were too talented not to be playing finals. There are also clear echoes here of Richmond in early 2017, and Collingwood in 2018 – clubs that backed their coach but tweaked the structures around them.

A new Head of AFL Performance role was created for Alan Richardson, the former Collingwood player and St Kilda coach. Alan is an astute thinker, and was put to work on a strategic view for the side, looking for fresh ideas. Mark 'Choco' Williams, the former Collingwood player and Port Adelaide premiership coach, was sounded out to head up player development. The maverick coach had always been a passionate teacher of young men – combustible and flamboyant – an archetype we didn't really have beforehand. And finally, Adem Yze was brought back to the club. He was once a favourite son, gone for almost a decade, but he wasn't brought back out of romance. He was lured away from Hawthorn because he's a bright mind with a cool head and calm delivery.

I remember the day 'Ooze' signed with the club, he sent a text to the midfield group. He would be at a cafe, My Other Brother, in Camberwell, in case anyone wanted to come along. We had a full showing. It wasn't just Ooze who wanted to talk about what we could improve, either – it was the midfield itself. We touched on what our best football looks like, and of course it's when we're playing as a unit. We have stars. Multiple stars. And they could continue to be stars. So long as the end product was a star midfield unit. I always say this about Richmond: Dusty is their gun, but he plays the way Damien Hardwick wants him to play, and he plays the way Trent Cotchin *needs* him to play. Christian Petracca and Clayton Oliver are stars, and yes, they need James Harmes and Jack Viney and Tom Sparrow to bring what they do, but Trac and Clarry have got to play their role and give back to the group, too. We told Ooze all of that – what we thought was wrong with our midfield and what could get better – and it was all mirrored by him. He had read us – perfectly – from the outside.

Our high performance manager and fitness boss, Darren Burgess' is the best in the business, and one of his findings from the 2020 season was that we needed to make sure everyone trains. Burgess has a saying he rattles off frequently: 'There's more to give.' If you're cramping, there's more to give. If you've got an injury, remember that part of it is mental, because there's more to give. We needed to make sure that everyone trained to a higher level than before. And soon enough, we got to this point where everyone wanted to train every session, and you look back now at what happened: we got to grand final week and we had all 45 players doing our main session. It became infectious.

But there were still these lingering questions hanging over our heads. Our fans couldn't trust us. They wanted to know who we were. Were we the team that surged into a preliminary final in 2018? Or the side that utterly collapsed under the weight of that rise (and injury), falling to third bottom in 2019? Or were we a bit of both, deserving of our middling ninth place finish in 2020? Members would ask our coach that question the most – *Are we far away from again cresting that wave?* – and Simon Goodwin gave them his answer. 'Not far away at all,' he told them. The foundations were laid. The expectations were raised. 'We don't want to just play finals,' he said at the time. 'We want to play significant finals and win significant finals.'

Goody lives on the Mornington Peninsula as well. We live only a few streets away from one another, so I got to see him up close and personal as he was making these declarations. I can only say this one way: he turned full footy nuffy. In an off-season where I was trying to reset and recharge, getting away from it all, Goody was trying to win us a flag in October. Honestly, I felt like saying, 'Can't you just let me watch the Caulfield Cup in peace?' But the amount of conversations we had over a coffee or a beer, on a walk or around the campfire, even going for a run around Rye Oval, I'm so glad that we were able to do that. He would share his ideas and philosophies, and I could tell him the players' perspective and how we might feel, and in that way we were able to get where we wanted. We found something. And it was presented on day one of pre-season training.

Every year we have a goal. Let's do better than we did last year. Let's make the top eight. Let's make the top four. It's always relative, and general. This year Goody went specific. 'We're winning it,' he said. 'We're winning it all.' That's the first year that's happened. He put it right up on the big screen down at Casey Fields. We sat down in the auditorium and up there the words sat in big bold letters: 'MISSION: GRAND FINAL DAY.' He explained what we needed to do, and how to do it, and it all circled back to this new trademark we adopted. Our trademark for 2021 was going to be 'TRUE' – Trust, Respect, Unity and Excellence – and TRUE applied to everyone, from the president to the bootstudder.

What did Trust mean for the guys? Playing your role. Unity? Being together, and celebrating the small things. Respect? That meant respecting the game, the opposition, the task you're up against – even the past and what the club has gone through. Excellence? That was the new part. I loved it.

There's something about pre-season messaging. It's often really familiar. Sometimes you would swear it was taken from one of those inspirational, motivational posters – recycled and trotted out in a different format every summer. In footy, 'playing your role' was always that thing. I'm 29 years old, so I've been playing footy in one form or another for more than two decades, and I've lost count of the number of times a coach implored me to play my role. Do your job and we win, do your part and we prevail, be that cog in the machine and the day is ours. But this wasn't just about playing your role. It was a clearer directive. Be *excellent* at your role. Be *elite* at your role. Be the *best* at your role. Look at Ed Langdon. He plays his role to an absolute T, as a wingman who runs up and down the ground, over and over, indefatigable, owning the far side of the MCG. But to be excellent at his role, he needed to address his kicking, and so he went away and worked on that craft, and then he became an *excellent* winger, still running up and down, still playing that role, only now kicking goals and cutting teams open.

Goody would have gone over that mission statement a thousand times, backspacing and clearing it all and punching it out again, and he nailed it. And the next time we got together as a playing group, we all sort of sat back and thought 'How fucking good is it that our coach has put a grand final on the board for us? We've just finished ninth, but we're talking about excellence.' He just got all of the players straight away, on day one.

It wasn't long before we got together again as a club, too, for a golf day at Settlers Run Golf & Country Club in Cranbourne. We had a shotgun start, with staff and players in a big competition. Days out like that are needed to break up the summer months. All that focus can get awfully serious. You need a bit of light at times. Luke Jackson provided that. Par for the course is 72, and Jacko had 200 shots. He would have had more, but picked up his ball 16 times, only actually finishing two holes. He was just *phenomenally* bad. I came second that day. Steven May won it all. And I remember we had a presentation for the new staff.

Adem Yze got up and spoke. There was a new head physiotherapist, Dan James. A new head of strength and conditioning, Selwyn Griffith. A new VFL coach, Mark Corrigan. Choco Williams got up and offered a six-slide presentation about winning flags and beating cancer and meeting Princess Diana – just this wild ride of pages and pages of pure-gold life story. And then our new doctor, Jacob Jewson, who's 29 and has been studying for half his life, gets up with one page, and it's about the time he went to see The Ashes, because he enjoys cricket, and how he loves *World of Warcraft*. He's never met Princess Di. Following Choco just wasn't fair.

None of these voices in and of themselves were the source of pivotal change. That's an important thing to note in football. There's so much exchange between clubs – of players and coaches and personnel all through these sprawling organisations – that you rarely find one person entering and making a crashing, undeniable impact. What you get though, particularly when six or seven new faces appear, is incremental change. The new voices aren't better than the old ones, but they are new, and, at least in Choco's case, they are different. And these new voices create a new energy, and they bring new methods, and new personalities and intelligences. It's like doing a new workout when the old one feels a bit staid. Sometimes you need something different, to trick the muscles and keep them guessing. Change is good. It's something you can't fear. You need to appreciate it and welcome it, even if it involves you, which one day it will. My turn will come, when the club needs change and needs me to move on. I hope when it does I can feel I played my part.

Once the staff had left that day, the players stayed. And we had this three-hour session about what we wanted to learn from 2020. Sporting organisations do this kind of thing all the time. They call it add-keep-delete, or stop-start-maintain. We talked along those lines, all 45 of us, about what we wanted to stand for, and how we could create an environment that made us happy to come to work each day. The main thing was to be more selfless. That sounds so clichéd, because we've had that discussion every year. Every bloody club has that discussion every bloody year. Everyone wants to be the best teammate they can be, but how do we actually do that, and how do we make ourselves accountable if we waver?

It was a really good discussion, and I remember that it wasn't just me and Jack Viney and Nathan Jones. First-year players spoke. Recruits spoke. People went way off on tangents, and people stayed focused, and people went at each other. Often when you see a disagreement in these settings, it looks good. It looks productive and necessary, like steel sharpening steel. But when you're the one in the middle of the disagreement, you can get worked up. As the hours went by, I'm sure some were thinking that they had had these same discussions every year, but nothing ever changes.

But if you're really going to change for good – so you don't keep going around and around in some downward spiral – you have to find common goals. You have to find each other. We all had to do that, with 45 sets of eyes watching us. It was 9 pm by the time we left, and people were almost falling asleep, but no-one regretted it. Because it was in these sorts of sessions that we really unpicked what we were doing wrong.

We talked about selfishness and what that looks like. It was obvious. Selfishness was when one midfielder would get 40 disposals, and another would only get 20 and be bitter about the guy who got 40. Selfishness was two guys competing for the same mark. Selfishness was those moments in the contest where the game is slipping away and a star tries to slip on his Superman cape to win the match himself, rather than blocking or tackling or shepherding or doing that one little thing he needed to do in that one little contest to make that nearby teammate that little bit better. Those things – getting 40 touches, taking the soaring mark, strapping the team on your back and carrying everyone alone – can be intoxicating for a star player. But if the byproduct of that thrill isn't winning, what's the point? I'm as guilty as anyone. I've flown for the grab when I shouldn't have. And now? Staying grounded and watching Jake Lever take the mark that could be mine is what brings me happiness.

After those meetings, everything began to feel better than it had in quite some time. But you can't let that fool you, either. December, January and February – these are the easy months of football. You don't have to stand by what you said at the end of October in those months, because there's no pressure, no newspaper articles, no stress of performance – of fans, of friends, of mum and dad calling you after a big session or game to see how you went. The important part was going into matches. We've made changes in the past that felt good, like we were motoring along in a groove, only to play a match and find that we were actually stuck in a rut. A loss will bring you down quickly, while a win affirms everything.

There's a chicken-and-egg question here: When you get on a hot streak – as we eventually did – was it the culture that came first and created the wins, or did the winning make the culture real? Did the way we changed help us win 9 and 0, or did winning 9 and 0 help us change? I'm inclined to think they both help each other. And in that context, the pre-season games mattered to us. People might think these games don't count, but they do. And in 2021 both our JLT games were important in different ways.

Richmond came first. We played the reigning premiers at 9.30 am on a Thursday in late February, and they put a very good team on the park, at least for the first three quarters. And we beat them, and that gave us confidence, because of the manner in which we did things. All those little behaviours we talked about were on show. It gave us belief that what we said we wanted to do was something we would be able to deliver. It was good to see it, and taste it, and know that it worked.

And then we got a massive reality check. We came in against the Bulldogs not long after, with confidence sky high, and we went away from everything we had pledged, and we got murdered. There was a nine-day gap between games, but it felt like we had forgotten everything, because we got big heads, because we were fools floating sky high over winning a midweek scratch match.

But in a way, that became almost perfect. That Western Bulldogs game set us up for the early weeks of the home-and-away season. We constantly referred to that game. Even as far into the season as Round 5, we would be chatting at half-time when the match was in the balance and going, 'But remember the Doggies game.'

There were these constant references. No-one would think a practice game could have that effect on a group, but it did.

There was one final thing that happened in the pre-season, right near the end, which I think was important. People signed up. Before the season itself had begun, and then through the early months of the year, important names signed important contracts. Jake Lever. Christian Petracca.

Clayton Oliver. Christian Salem. That gave me so much confidence that the group was happy – that an environment had been created that people wanted to stay in.

We don't have the greatest facilities. If you live in Melbourne you have an hour-long drive to Casey, for four main sessions a week. And you don't get to call that one place home – we split facilities by also training at AAMI Park. If you did a league ranking, our facilities would probably be last, and yet we kept all these people. It was like we could all see where we were going, like there was something we could just make out on the horizon, and it wasn't a mirage.

I was happy to sign on myself, on a four-year contract extension that would tie me to the club until the end of 2025. I was always going to be a Demon for life. It was an easy decision. But there's ego on your shoulder, too. Your manager wants you to get the best deal possible, and you want to set your family up, but you also know that for us to keep Petracca, Oliver, Lever, May – and everyone else – you've gotta do your bit. Sometimes you need to convince others, but I never needed to convince myself.

The Melbourne Football Club was speaking so loudly in my ears. We have a great history but a poor recent history, and I wanted to be involved with the team that changed all that for good. We all did. It's not 20/20 hindsight to say we felt we were on the verge of something.

We knew we had the skills. We knew we had the fitness. We knew we had a gameplan. We had every position on the field covered – elite talent on every line. And there was belief, too – so much belief. Confidence was never the issue. Attitude was.

That summer, we emerged into autumn feeling as though we had stronger minds and harder heads, like there was no pressure we couldn't handle, no support we couldn't offer to each other, and no wall we couldn't break through as one.

At the main training session before Round 1 against the Dockers, we stood in a circle in the middle of the oval, and we did what we do every pre-season session – we had a good long chat. We talked about what we saw, what we liked, pinpointing a few people and a few deeds. This was our last session before the season proper, and it felt so crucial to start one and zero rather than zero and one, so I spoke to the boys about that. What I said was this: 'We're winning this week. We're beating Fremantle. And after that, we're never leaving the eight.'

CHAPTER 2

Round 1

Saturday March 20, 1:45pm
Melbourne Cricket Ground
Melbourne (11.14.80) versus Fremantle (8.10.58)

It's strange that it feels remarkable now, but the most remarkable thing about playing the Dockers in Round 1 at the MCG was the normality of it all. There were 21,365 people at the home of football, about what you would expect against an interstate club. Fremantle had come from Western Australia with no need to quarantine – not even the threat of needing to quarantine. It was early autumn and still warm. Just another day at the footy, the start of a regular season, as if the Australian Football League had finally returned to normal.

I was playing against a debutant – Lloyd Meek – which I tend to find puts a bit of pressure on me. When you play directly opposite someone young and you're the mature footballer of the two, there's an expectation that you should dominate. That's particularly true of senior ruckmen – this notion that all those pre-seasons and weights sessions and time trials will easily see you over the line against someone who's green.

But I've got an immense ruck knowledge. I study all of these guys all across the competition, and so the average footy fan might not know who Lloyd Meek is, but I knew all about him. I'm a great fan of the kid, and knew it wouldn't be as easy against him as it might have looked to some. He may have been only 22, but don't let that fool you, he was 111 kilograms, as solid as a rock. I really didn't have the best day.

James Harmes had a pretty good day. He was playing on Brownlow medalist Nat Fyfe, and managed to quell him a little while getting 20 touches and a goal himself – a good day at the office for any midfielder. If he had a good day, then Tom McDonald had a great day. After an amazing pre-season – perhaps the best among the entire playing group – Tom held down the forward line as our lone tall option, running up and back, helping himself to 18 possessions, nine marks and two goals. Clayton Oliver was dominant, with 35 disposals and seven clearances in his 100th game, beginning his steady march to Brownlow favouritism. He got the three votes, in fact, which I think possibly proves it's a midfielders' medal, because the guys

I thought would fight it out for best on ground were Jake Lever and Steven May, our twin towers in defence.

Their numbers were stark. Lever had 18 touches, including 9 contested possessions and a career-high six intercept marks. May had 24 touches to go with eight grabs of his own. Coach Simon Goodwin talked about it afterwards. When asked how they had won, he was brief: 'Command from behind the ball.' You could see that what that pair had been talking about in their defensive meetings all pre-season long was working.

But it was also as if Jake and Steve had chosen the first game of the year to make a swift statement – that the Demons would be the stingiest defence in the competition. That's how the season unfolded, with 1443 total points against us (an average of 65 per game) – the lowest tally in the league. In many ways those two guys became the bedrock on which this season was built. I remember thinking at the time, 'Those two are up and going – they're set.'

They came to Melbourne not far apart. Jake came first, immediately after playing for Adelaide in the 2017 Grand Final. When I first got told we were getting him, it was at our post-season recruiting meeting, and Josh Mahoney (then general manager of Football Operations) said, 'This guy is a ready-made leader, almost a ready-made captain – he's a star, and you're gonna love him.'

But my first dealings with Jake didn't give me that impression. It was hard to pin down, but my reflection was that he had a lot of growing up to do – that he wasn't a ready-made leader or ready-made captain. He was just a bit immature, and if you ask him about it now, he thinks he was, too. There was an inconsistency around his habits. These days he seems like a 30-year-old – even though he's 25 – or maybe even a 50-year-old at times. But back then he just seemed young. I guess he was, too. He was only 21.

Jake grew up on a farm in Lancefield, near Romsey, and was thrown into the backline in interleague games as a kid, where he tried to make that part of the ground his own. That happens sometimes in footy – you find your space on the oval and stay there. As you go up through the ranks – and he did this with Vic Metro – it gets consolidated. Backman for life.

He was drafted by the Crows at pick 14, even though he was coming off a knee injury, and put together three years that were hard not to notice in a young player, named to the All Australian squad of 40 and playing in a grand final. He came to us, ruptured his anterior cruciate ligament halfway through his first season as a Demon in 2018, and missed our entire dream run to the preliminary final that year. It's easy to see what drives him, and he is definitely driven.

He's now one of my closest mates and one of my favourite teammates. He's got incredible habits, training literally every session. He's big on getting the same level out of Jake Lever every single week, and that's just such a great quality to have.

He has his quirks, as do we all. Jake does float tanks – sensory deprivation almost, in a closed watery pod – and he *has* to do it the night before every game. He floats in a tank for an hour, completely silent. It doesn't matter if we're playing interstate, he'll try to work out where in Perth he can go to do a float tank for an hour the night before we play. It may seem a bit weird, but I think it's like meditation for him, releasing all your thoughts and becoming one with yourself.

I'm not big on it, but I am big on what it shows: that he knows what to do to get the best out of himself, and he's willing to go and do it. He now is exactly what Josh Mahoney said he was to me on day one – that ready-made leader, a captain in the making.

Steven May is nothing like him, incidentally, but I mean that in the best possible way. I remember meeting Steve for the first time not long after that preliminary final, at Simon Goodwin's house just after our Mad Monday of 2018. It was me, Nathan Jones, Jake Lever, and our list manager, Tim Lamb. There were whispers around that time that Steve might go to Collingwood, but we had a chat at Goody's place and I knew then that we were going to get him. It was clear that he liked the idea of the partnership with Jake, a real one–two punch. And it was also clear that he was a real competitor.

But I guess I knew him more as an angry stay-at-home defender, tough and uncompromising. I hadn't seen his attacking flair. Not everyone eats, sleeps and breathes the game, and Steve is a guy who needs a life away from footy to play his best footy.

We saw that best footy in 2020, when he made the All Australian squad of 40, and was unlucky not to be named in the team. He's in our leadership group now because of the way he performs – what he brings to us on field. Steve is so *demanding* out there. You can hear him all over the field. Trent Rivers and Jake Bowey are actually scared of him, but we get the best out of Trent Rivers and Jake Bowey because of him. I know what it's like to be in their boots, because in my role I sometimes have to come back and play on Steve's man, sitting behind the ball, freeing him up. If I let his man kick a goal on me, I don't even look at him, because I know what's coming. And I think it's so important to have a full-back like that – with this will to win and refusal to be scored against. It means every goal the opposition kicks is going to be deserved.

But of course their strength as a defensive pair is more than the way they shut down, rather it's the way they repel. That's where one of those misconceptions creeps in, that neither one plays too closely on a man. That they have pure freedom. To an extent they do have freedom. But if it's true that the team can't do without Lever and May, it's equally true that Lever and May can't do without the team. They need Jayden Hunt or Ed Langdon or Gus Brayshaw to fold back from the wing. They need Joel Smith or Adam Tomlinson or Harrison Petty to stand beside the most dangerous forwards. It all requires cooperation and coordination. We call it playing as 'one and a half men', where two guys keep an eye each on the same opponent, and their other eye on the play. They need all the moving parts to succeed, even our midfield.

We weren't by any means dominant in Round 1. In truth we got beaten out of the middle. But we did it differently than in the past. We got beaten out of the middle in a good way. Getting beaten out of the middle in a bad way is allowing Nat Fyfe or Andrew Brayshaw or Caleb Serong to stream out of the centre square with their eyes lowered on a leading forward, with only clear air between them. We didn't allow them to do that. We lost clearances – but only scrappy ones. They got free – but only off the back of the stoppage. They got kicks away forward – but only high balls that are easy to kill. And when you combine that pressure in tandem with talent like Lever and May, you're starting in a really good place.

It's thrilling to watch them when they're in full flight, as they were against the Dockers. It's as though Lever has been honing that ability to come off his man since he was a teenager. He calculates the ball in the air, judging risk versus reward, and commits to that intercept. While May has that ability to stand beside the monster forward, the bear in the square, and fight to win his one-on-one with superior positioning and strength. Combined, they become a single entity at times. The interceptor and the stopper. The past captain and future captain.

They make things look easy and clean, but the game itself wasn't like that. This was that classic windy game at the 'G, everything a little scattered and messy. Sometimes in the early part of a season that's the way it is, as you find your feet and your form. Not every game is a blockbuster or a blowout. Sometimes getting the four points feels ugly – and sometimes that's necessary. That's what good teams do. They win ugly, and get it done.

After the game, I thought back to that final training session a few days earlier, when we had our chat in the centre of the ground at Casey Fields. You always know your messages are being received when people refer back to them later. And that's what happened here. I remember after that Dockers game, in the basement of the MCG, you could tell people were thinking only of how we had ticked that first box. 'Started with a win, Maxy,' a few of the guys said to me. 'Now we stay in the eight. Off we go.'

CHAPTER 3

Round 2

Saturday March 27, 7:25pm

Marvel Stadium

St Kilda (11.7.73) versus Melbourne (12.19.91)

I've played professional football for a dozen years now, and have a lot of experience starting seasons poorly, so it was great to start this season well, with back-to-back wins for the first time in four years. It was a night game at Marvel Stadium, and we beat St Kilda by three goals, although it wasn't actually three goals. In truth we beat them by one goal and 12 behinds. It was that sort of contest, riddled with errors and marked by long, frustrating stretches when poor conversion threatened to undo a lot of good work.

Clayton Oliver was superb again, followed closely by the Christians – Petracca and Salem – and Tom McDonald continued to repay faith and restore trust, not just with the players, but supporters, too. The highlight came from a

19-year-old kid playing his 16th match. I'll talk more about Kysaiah Pickett later, but he kicked two goals that night, and one of them became a contender for goal of the year. We love Kozzy for the forward pressure he applies and opportunities he creates for others, but it's also impossible not to sit back and give thanks when he does what he did in the second quarter, roving off a pack, dancing through traffic, slipping past tackles and finishing on the left. He kicked the sealer in the last quarter, too, and shortly afterward Goody told media that he had already become one of those players supporters will pay to come and watch, and he's not wrong.

But the person I really want to talk about in this round is Angus Brayshaw, and not because of the way he played. In fact, he had just 13 touches, almost his quietest game for the season in terms of sheer statistical output. But here's the thing – that's not necessarily a poor game for him, although it would be easy to see it that way if you're looking in from the outside, and still thinking about a stellar season he once had. In 2018 Gus finished third in the Brownlow Medal. But our team at the time had too many inside midfielders. People in the media could see it, and other teams could, too. There were moments that analysts could pick apart and see five Demon mids swarming to the stoppage – see ball, get ball, like bees to the honeypot – with not enough numbers back a few metres on the outside. It's what's called 'lacking balance in the contest'. A consequence of that is Gus now accepting a less flashy role, in which he spends large chunks of every game – practically the entire game – on the wing. He became a winger because we needed a winger.

But what did that do to his football? Numbers only ever tell part of the story, but sometimes they're stark. In 2018 Gus averaged 26.1 possessions and 4.3 clearances per game, and kicked 14 goals. This year? Those numbers dropped to 18.1 possessions, 1.4 clearances and three goals. We talked about selfishness and selflessness in the pre-season. Often that means embodying team traits, training as you should, developing good habits, or making sure you do all the hard and necessary things on field, to put your teammate in a better position. But other times it means making a genuine *sacrifice* – your game, for the team game. That's what Gus did.

And it became this utter strength of ours. We suddenly had one winger who was an extremely good runner and outside player in Ed Langdon, and another winger who was the opposite – an extremely good inside player and decision-maker in Angus – and they drove one another to be better at overcoming their weaknesses, to the point that Ed is now someone who can get involved in clearances, and Gus can get back to help our defenders with close–out spoils.

His new role meant there would be games where he might only get nine touches, and supporters would be calling for his head, while internally we were almost giving him our best player of the week. That's tricky – understanding and accepting that the only praise he was going to get was from us. Remember, he knew he could do more. Much more. The only people ahead of him in the Brownlow in 2018 were Steele Sidebottom and the guy with the medal, Tom Mitchell. You're in rare air when you're only 22 years old and you can out-poll Dustin Martin, Patrick Dangerfield and Brodie Grundy.

But he parked his ego – and that's the hardest thing to do as an elite athlete. He's talked about this before, and told people that it's easy to do when you can see the tangible results – how the weight of winning helps – but I still imagine it's something he thinks about when he's at home alone, or speaking to loved ones. All I can say is that having an example like that at the club – *and that's exactly what he was, an example for others* – was so valuable to us.

He had to do hard work to get there, too, not just mental but physical. Gus can clearly run, but the running a wingman does is different than an inside midfielder, and he came into the year off a very low base. Gus was injured in late 2020 and missed the final games of the season – he flew home from the hub early for an operation on the ligaments under his foot, meaning he was in rehabilitation until well into the new year. He missed almost the whole pre-season and had gained a little weight because of that. His pledge was to get fit, to be the highest-standard midfielder, and his way of doing that was an extra 'off-legs' session every week, for the whole year.

An off-legs session is basically a one-hour circuit, where you're not running but using heavy ropes and rowing and any other intense work that doesn't put training load through the feet. He decided this session would be a 6.30 am start, when you normally don't have to be at Casey Fields until maybe 8.30 am. So it was a demanding early wake up, given how far away Casey is. He called it 'win the morning, win the day'. And he brought a group with him. It transformed him back into an elite midfielder, but it also transformed our culture – into one that was determined to help someone get where they needed to go. We all thought Gus would quit it once he lost his weight and was back training, but he never did. It just grew into this thing. Pretty soon 'Win the Morning' had grown into a group that had 30 guys coming along. We did it all the way up to Grand Final week, when we had 45 guys doing the circuit at Joondalup Resort, around the pool.

The other reason to mention Gus here is the game itself. It was an emotional night. The Saints were staging the inaugural Spud's Game, in memory of the late Danny

Frawley, who passed away in mental distress as a result of concussion–related issues that stemmed from his playing career. Angus of course had a lot of concussions himself. In 2016 and 2017 he had four concussions in 12 months, including two in a three-week period. It was scary, for him and everyone who knew him. Even for those who didn't. He was a different person, and he seriously thought about stepping away from footy. But he also needed to play footy. When you're young, your footy is your identity – you *need* to be playing. He wears a helmet now, and it marks him as 'the concussion guy', but it's not even mentioned at the club. He's so far past it. Think of his Grand Final performance and his head-first attacks on the ball – he was our hardest player.

I like to remember a different game against St Kilda, in 2017, when he was coming back from those concussions. There was this massive contest – *just massive* – and there was a collision, and Gus ended up on the deck. And I could just hear the MCG, that way it sometimes goes silent, and you know people are gasping or sighing, and they're waiting. I was first on the scene, and I picked him up by the jumper and rubbed his head, and he gave me a little smile. And that's the last I've heard of it or thought of it. He needed that effort. He knows the helmet does nothing, but he goes by this message: If I punched you in the head right now, and I said you can have this helmet on, would you rather have it, or not? And he says he'd rather have the helmet, and that's all there is to it.

He's a very good communicator, Gus. He's in the leadership group this year. He's a good friend, a very funny person. And one other thing to note about this round – perhaps the biggest thing to note – is his connection to 'Spud' Frawley. Angus's girlfriend is Danielle Frawley, Danny's daughter. She was with us in the hub last year. And you remember that what we created in that hub was a sense of family? Danielle was absolutely a part of that. She was accepted and embraced almost like she was a player. She actually did play women's footy, too, and got concussed. In juniors, Danny was her coach. So what that week meant for Angus, and what it meant for Danielle, inspired us to a level where it felt as though we had as much invested in the game as St Kilda. Round 2 felt like a shared round.

I do a podcast with Angus – *Gus and Gawny* – and Danielle came and spoke to us, and I was utterly moved by this cause, of mental health and concussion and men connecting more honestly with each other, and what Spud meant to Danielle and to Angus. And Danielle spoke the day before the game – 'Time to Talk' was the slogan. And we really all felt something as a group. We wanted to play for the Frawley family.

In the captain's run meeting – after the final session of the week – Gus used that moment to talk to the 23 who were suiting up that week, and he encouraged everyone in that room to call someone on the way home. A mate of mine was going through a divorce, and I called him. Goody called someone really important to him. Everyone called someone who was going through a rough trot.

Gus wasn't just saying to us that it was a big game, very important, all that stuff you hear so often – he was demanding *action*. The target in these campaigns is males, as it should be. We don't talk enough. We don't ask after our mates enough. Gus was saying to us that we play football and pretend that we're too cool to talk, and that's not bloody good enough.

Before the game, we had Garry Lyon and Tony Lockett come out and speak to us all as we were linking arms before the bounce. I don't know about the other players, but it all hit me then. None of that has anything to do with why you win or lose, because the message was for the Saints as much as it was for the Dees. But I do know that I looked at Gus, and knew how he'd poured his heart out, and I just felt like, 'Yeah, I'm in this. This means something. This week I'm going to give him everything I can.'

CHAPTER 4

Round 3

Sunday April 4, 6:10pm

Manuka Oval

Greater Western Sydney (11.2.68) versus Melbourne (15.12.102)

Greater Western Sydney are always thereabouts on the ladder. Even when they're wounded, you can never quite trust in the result against them, given their talent and system. They were already hurt going into this game, missing Lachie Whitfield and Jesse Hogan, and then they lost Stephen Coniglio, Phil Davis and Matt de Boer to injury during the match. They had lost their first two games of the season as well, so they were desperate, and it showed.

Despite their talent missing from the field, sitting in the grandstands or on the sideline, the Giants kicked three of the first four goals, and they surged back against us in the last quarter, too, before we finally pulled clear. I had one of my best games of the season, but I was more focused on the fact that we had now won three from three. I was also focused on a young player in our forward line.

It would be wrong to say that this was the breakout game for Kysaiah Pickett, because it's not at all the first time he's lit up a footy field for us. But there's something about a player backing up one good game with another, and another – as Kozzy was doing, and continued to do all year – that makes you take notice. He kicked four that night in Canberra. One in the third quarter was an instant inclusion in his highlights reel – creating the turnover, plucking from the deck and snapping truly. Sometimes he makes you smile or laugh over what he can do. And the way he plays is made more remarkable by his story.

That's all been pretty well reported already, as has the way he arrived on the scene last year. What I think about most, though, is what happened at the start of this season. Kozzy dazzled everyone that night in Canberra against the Giants, and he looked like pure joy out there, but he was so far away from that only two months before.

It was just prior to the season, and his mother Rebecca – the aunty who adopted him – died. In February he was given permission to return to Perth to mourn, but to get into Western Australia he had to do two weeks of quarantine in Adelaide. No-one really knew how he would cope with that. Under those circumstances, it would be fair for any kid to curl up and cry. I'm sure he did. But the first thing I remember seeing was these videos of him training.

There was a guy over there in South Australia, Paul Vandenbergh, who runs the AFL's national diversity pathway program, and he was working with him. He captured this vision of Kozzy doing F45 workouts. He was getting up at 5 am to do kicking sessions, and running sessions, and the videos were coming through to Darren Burgess, who posted them on a WhatsApp group. That stuff just cut through immediately with his teammates. To some guys, it was the making of him.

For a 19-year-old to be away from home, with that kind of grief hanging over him, and to play the footy that he did – I just found that so giving. And mature. That he could park that family stuff – deep, close family stuff – and get back here and stay in the system, and not just perform but *star* – I'm in awe. In his first three games, people were talking about him as an All Australian small forward, and he looked every bit of that and more.

I'm grateful for the people around him. Melbourne has surrounded him with support from the beginning, whether that's Indigenous welfare boss Matthew Whelan, or forwards coach Greg Stafford, or player development manager Shannon Byrnes. He lived with Neville Jetta in the early days, and now he lives with Christian Petracca. He's close to Toby Bedford and Charlie Spargo.

I'm also proud of the way the club was with him, giving him that time and understanding. Throughout the year, whenever we thought there was a chance between COVID interruptions for him to get home and see family, we got him home to see family, and it's those kinds of gestures and efforts that let you know your organisation is on the right path.

And then, of course, you reap the rewards. He really just began to put it all together. He kicked what could have been the goal of the year against St Kilda in Round 2, but in Round 3, well, just pull up a chair.

I remember thinking I'd played quite well, and was pretty pleased with myself. I was walking off the ground ready for people to pat me on the back, but everyone just went straight to Kozzy. Toby Greene was the highlight at the other end of the ground, and he's one of the best players in the competition, but Toby didn't shine any more brightly than Kozzy. He's a special talent.

It's clear that he has speed, either to get to contests or stream away from them. But wheels will only get you so far in football. He also works incredibly hard to win one-on-ones. And sometimes the most impressive thing is how he can put it all together in a sequence. It's one thing to sprint to a contest, another to win it, and yet another to sprint clear afterwards. The finishing touch is sometimes the hardest part. Exhausted from the effort, players are often spent and then crumble at that last crucial moment, but he finishes. He has this surprising reserve of energy. And I think the coaching staff know that about him.

They kept experimenting with Kozzy in the pre-season. They were playing him in the midfield a lot, trying to build his tank, and I remember thinking, this is interesting. We've got certain drills, for instance, where it's 12 versus 12, but one player wears a bib and they play offence for *both* teams, running up and down the length of the ground. They were giving that role to Kozzy, and again I remember thinking, this is interesting.

Jordan Lewis was a coach with us in the pre-season, before COVID meant he had to choose between that and his jobs in media. And Jordan came up to me one session and said, 'I've seen Cyril Rioli at training today ... and he's wearing a Melbourne jumper.' That's a lot of praise. But then when you watch Kozzy play, in the heat of the moment, it's all too clear. His kick to Ben Brown in the first minutes of the preliminary final – the way he tapped it around a player, scooted behind, gathered and drilled this perfectly weighted pass – that's such dazzling flair.

But he combines that with an ability to be the role player we require. He does all the things a pressure forward needs to do, whether occupying space or closing up exit routes. He's a star, but he's part of a brigade. Charlie Spargo and Kozzy – two of them in the one team, and one unit, led by Alex Neal-Bullen. They never all dominate at once, because they need each other to sacrifice so one can get the lick of the cream. In the GWS game, Spargo and Neal-Bullen did what they needed to do, and that allowed Kozzy to do his best work.

And his best work is something to watch. We want our players to find those moments when they can be themselves. We want them to express who they are through their footy. We want Trac to be Trac. We want Clayton to be Clayton. Yes, they have to tick off what we want in terms of being TRUE – *Trust, Respect, Unity, Excellence* – but beyond that, let them be who they are.

Put it this way, if Kozzy has the ball on the boundary, goal in his sights, and there's someone inside but he takes his shot anyway, you go up to him later and tell him there was someone inside.

But you also want him to take his shot if he thinks it's there. After all, they usually go in, or almost do. Take that away from him and what else are you taking away? What else do you miss out on? I say let Kozzy be Kozzy.

CHAPTER 5

Round 4

Sunday April 11, 3:20pm

Melbourne Cricket Ground

Melbourne (12.13.85) versus Geelong (9.6.60)

Our first three games of the year were against very good opposition. Fremantle are young, and younger sides are better early in the year – more dangerous before the length and rigours of the season wears them down a little. St Kilda were finalists the year prior, and we were playing them on their deck, before the win/loss ledger dashed their hopes of ending up in the eight again. GWS are always around the mark, and put up a resistance that was half talent and half determination. But still, Round 4 against Geelong felt like it would be different.

These boys were battle hardened. They were the oldest team in the competition, and when you come up against that, what you notice first is abundant physical strength and conditioning. Second, you feel the weight of all that experience, in decision-making, poise and a clear understanding of their system. Basically, they have bodies and minds that are honed – prepared and ready to grind you down. Externally, we also had people telling us 'You're three and zero, but who have you played?' Well, now we were playing Geelong, the flag favourites.

It was a big game for us – a litmus test at the MCG, still in front of crowds. The game was built up well by the football media, but also by us, as a chance to take a real scalp. As footballers, we tell the world that external commentary is meaningless noise, not so much ignored as not even heard. But it does seep in sometimes, and when it does it provides you with perspective.

We were jacked up for this one, and we won by 25 points. We put a couple of goals on the board late, too – it was a far closer match than the four-goal margin would suggest. That's why it stood out to us as such an important performance. The game was tight and yet it felt like we were in control all throughout the twilight. It was the first time we've won four games to start the season since 1994. We were ticking boxes, managing the outcome, and playing front-half footy, keeping the ball close to our goals, without fully clicking as a forward line.

All the way up until the end of the year there were questions about the shape of our attack, from where Ben

Brown and Sam Weideman sat in the pecking order, to the best path toward goal. Goalkicking seemed to be an issue again and again, and yet goalkicking is something we've worked on incredibly hard. Greg Stafford was my ruck coach for six years, and is now the forward line, goalkicking and ruck coach. I hate sharing him with others. I get grumpy about not having him all to myself.

Goalkicking is really about working out what works for you. For me, writing out what I do, giving that to Staf, and then being expected to do that every time – *does not work*. I like to throw the ball around in my hands. Sometimes I count my steps and sometimes I don't. But I want the point of strike to be the same every week. And that's basically what he teaches. You do it your way, but your way has to stand up and be reproducible under extreme pressure. And so we have to train it under extreme pressure. You can't just have 100 set shots on your day off. That's handy. Repetition works. But more important are those moments after a big session, with everyone watching, and you're absolutely blowing steam after a two-minute effort, and Staf grabs you and says, 'OK, let's see what you can do on the angle from 40 metres out.' I also think he gets results because he's passionate and thoughtful about what he's doing. Greg Stafford could say, 'Good goalkicking is chipping it over your own head while blindfolded', and if he said it with enough heart the guys would believe him.

It was wet that day against Geelong, and they say that's when pure footballers shine. It sounds counterintuitive, as though sodden conditions would bring the game down to the lowest level, but it's the players with touch and power who shine brightest in the gloom. They don't fumble and they don't miss. Jimmy Bartel was a menace in the rain. James Hird rose to another level. It's a little bit like that with Christian Petracca. He had 36 touches, nine clearances, two goals and 657 metres gained.

Christian has always been a special talent – always obviously gifted – and he clearly also always knew he could turn it on. But there was a moment near the end of 2019 when I think things changed for him. Everyone was disappointed with the year, none more so than Christian. He got fifth in the best and fairest but he thought he should have been higher – thought he was undervalued. So he went away and said, 'Bugger it – I'm training my arse off. I'm going to show these guys I'm better than what they're saying.'

He came back in early 2020 and he was playing well, and understanding how to run through full games as a midfielder, but we were losing anyway, and I think at that point he realised he had gone a bit amiss – that we as a *group* have to say 'Bugger it'. I always knew at some point he was going to flick his fingers and play midfield, but playing the way he does, turning it on and leading this dynamic midfield with such ferocity – I didn't really know that was coming. This season snuck up on everyone.

What changed? Christian just grew up. He found his routines. He loves his mindfulness, but he didn't once – he's had to learn how. He's learned all these different habits that will make him the best Christian Petracca he can be. Andrew Waterson is our performance psychologist and mindfulness coach, and he talks to him, but Christian also works with people outside the club. We all have our own way. My mindfulness routine is driving. I drive an hour each way to training and I love it. That's my time away from anyone. On the highway, you zone out, and then you get home and open the door to your house and try to become the best husband you can be, the best son – soon the best father. Sometimes I listen to music, sometimes podcasts, but silence with the windows down is probably my favourite. And I think most players need that.

In the hub last year, Trac used to go to the beach alone. He's a social creature, but at 6.30 am he would go down there, not to jump in the water but just to have the sand under his feet, just to start his day the right way. That's maturity. Early Trac would have wanted to play basketball, then PlayStation, then basketball again, all before training – his mind and body working a million miles an hour. But he knows he's a leader now and he makes these demands of himself, and he has to, because his brilliance isn't going to happen without Jack Viney, James Harmes and Clayton Oliver doing what's expected of them. In the Geelong game, the Cats sent their tagger, Mark O'Connor, to Clayton. Trac understands that he only gets off the leash because of the quality around him.

When he first got to the club, though, he was an infuriating bundle of energy, always the loudest, always lighting up every room. And you want that to stay, so you have to create an environment where that's safe for him. You can imagine that an 18-year-old extrovert with irrepressible 24/7 energy might get on a few nerves, so he needed to temper that as well. He found that balance, insofar as he now knows *when* to be him. It's not about altering yourself but instead knowing when to show all of yourself, so you can still be part of something greater. I'm glad he hasn't completely changed. I sat next to him for eight hours straight at our signing day after the Grand Final, when they put all these jumpers and posters and photos and cheese boards in front of you, and he did not stop talking for the whole eight hours. I almost shot him. But it just shows that he's still Christian. Within this whole transformation to become this dangerous ballistic footballer, he's still Christian. And that puts a smile on my face.

Adem Yze has been important, too. I never played with Ooze – I missed him by about a year in my career – but I saw him play. I remember him as a flashy half-forward, and I remember it came to an abrupt end when he was about 30, after playing 226 games straight. If you speak to Melbourne fans, he's rated so highly, sitting in their top 10 with the likes of Stynes, Lyon, Neitz, Schwarz. It's a handy top 10. Ooze eventually left, and so did Jeff White, Simon Godfrey, Matty Whelan and Paul Wheatley, all just before I got there. And then I was there for the departures of James McDonald, Cam Bruce, Brad Miller and Brad Green. They got rid of some of the older guys, and I think we definitely made some mistakes. Most of these guys are connected with our really strong past players group, but Ooze wasn't, because for the past 10 years he's been with another club, coaching at Hawthorn.

When he came to coach our midfield at the start of this season, it was the first time I'd met him. He seemed quite unassuming – no extrovert – but smart. He's quite reserved, and sometimes I don't think he *knows* he's a good coach. His record and résumé stands up – four flags with the Hawks – but I'm not sure he understands deep down the effect he can have on young people. He has a great way of talking with millennials and connecting with them. He works best with a handful of guys, but he can command a room of 45, too. I've never heard him raise his voice. He can tell us how it is after we've lost, giving us those home truths when we need to hear them, but the art of on–field coaching is telling players how to fix a problem. He shows the clip of what you're doing wrong, but only when he has an easy fix that can be learned and implemented. He gets us in his little group, he gets his iPad out, and he shows you this stoppage, this exit, this block – and bang, how we can fix everything.

That kind of skill has been amazing for Christian, and they have a great relationship. When I wrote earlier that you really shouldn't bother doing 100 set shots on your day off, Trac actually does, and Ooze comes with him. Their bond would have to be the closest out of any player–coach relationship at the club. And it's happened this year.

We all use coaches differently. I don't necessarily need to know if my game was good. I know when my game was good. But Trac likes feedback, wants feedback, and *needs* feedback. He has to know when he was good and why he was good and how he can be good again, and the opposite. If his game has been poor, he wants to know exactly how, so it doesn't happen again. Those two catch up straight away after every game, and they're the first to talk and go through vision on Monday. If I ask Ooze, 'Can I get some vision?' he says, 'Yeah mate, just after Trac.' They're very strong.

Watching Christian Petracca up close is a great thing. I love watching Clayton because he does *freakish* things in a one-metre square, and I love watching Viney and Jones and Harmes because they're such bulls, who give no quarter and expect none either.

But watching Trac in full flight is something else. There's this sheer *power* through the hips and quads, and the way he uses the ground as a leverage point against opponents, who can't hold him as he streaks away, and the way he kicks the Sherrin like it said something bad about his mum. I know why everyone loves watching him shove and shimmy, and accelerate and disappear. He's the best show in town, and I've got the best ticket.

CHAPTER 6

Round 5

Momentum in footy is a funny thing. Sometimes you can sense it building and building until it finally shifts your way. Other times you don't have a clue it's about to swing, and can't even tell that it's swung until the goals on the scoreboard tick over and over and over. Then you know you're deep in it – that collective flow state.

That's how it was against Hawthorn in Round 5. They put us under the pump early – a nice mix of old campaigners and youthful exuberance catching us on the hop. They led by 10 points at quarter-time, two points at half-time, and trailed by only 10 points at three-quarter time. They got the first goal of the last quarter, too, closing to within four points. Their resistance was holding. Until … it wasn't.

It's hard to say what changed exactly. Four minutes into the final quarter, we were only six points up. I took a mark 50 metres out at the city end, and kicked a goal from the set shot – post high, through the centre, practice makes perfect sometimes – and we were 12 points up. A two-goal difference with almost a quarter to play doesn't sound like the moment the dam is about to burst, but it was our biggest lead of the day, and maybe the Hawks could sense that, or maybe we could. We piled on the next six goals in a hurry. We kicked 8.4 for the quarter. We won by 50 points.

I read later that it was all about our forward connection. In the first half, we had 30 inside 50s for four goals. In the second half, we had 30 inside 50s for 11 goals. Sometimes football is like that. Sometimes things just click. It was notable because it was the first time for the year that we were able to pile on the majors in a flurry – to break an opponent with our attack. Jonesy said later that the unit we were forming was becoming demonstrably better than our 2018 team, and it's hard to disagree when you're in the middle of that kind of surge. It felt unfamiliar then – scoring so heavily and so fast – but in the finals that became the way of all our wins.

I had fun that day rucking against their captain, big Ben McEvoy. Ed Langdon was dominant on his wing, kicking three goals. Salem and Oliver had 30 touches each. Petracca had 23 touches and a pair of goals, and Tommy McDonald had 22 and two himself.

But there were three other guys having fun out there, and I'm so happy for each of them, given their football journeys. You might call them our Bomber connection. Jake Melksham. Michael Hibberd. Mitch Brown. Our coach, Simon Goodwin, is connected to that group, too. He was an assistant coach at the Dons for four years, serving under both James Hird and Mark 'Bomber' Thompson. He was caretaker senior coach for the final round of 2013, after Hird was suspended. He came to Melbourne in late 2014 on a five-year deal, to serve as an assistant under Paul Roos, before taking over in 2017. And you could see instantly that he knew those three boys well – that he had a relationship with them beyond the Demons.

Goody knows better than anyone how to whack Melky into gear. And how to get the best from Hibbo. And how to treat Mitchy. He knows how to straddle that line between mateship and leadership, and make it work. It must be tough at times. Take his connection to Hibbo as an example. He's been his assistant coach for eight years, and now his senior coach for four years, and at some point he'll have to tell Hibbo his time is up. The better the player, the longer they play, the stronger the memories and the deeper the connection. That's a pretty extreme relationship – to be a longtime mate and a longtime mentor – a father figure and a boss. Imagine walking someone through their career, as someone you have to teach, then coach, then drop, then retire. I don't think I'll ever want to coach.

Jakey Melksham was the first of the three to arrive. He came to us in the 2015 trade period. He did a full pre-season with us and made an impression, but immediately before Round 1 he got told that season 2016 was wiped out for him. Gone. He was suspended for a year, along with all those other Bombers. I can't imagine what that was like. Some of those players travelled for a year. Some of them stayed at home and trained. What that must have done to him – coming to a new club and then being stripped of his chance at a fresh start. I don't know how he coped. His personality probably helped.

If you judged Jake Melksham solely on what he's like as a player, you would gravely misunderstand the man. I know I did. I remember chatting to him as soon as he came to the club, maybe even in the first week. 'I hated you,' I told him. 'Every time I picture Melbourne playing against Essendon, all I can picture is you fighting with Jack Trengove.' He plays that way, with this constant animosity. If you think you can see it on TV, it's something else up close. He's always right on that line, which is where you want some teammates – up on that edge, just this side of right, but not far away from wrong. That's where some players find their best footy.

He's a very good player, and has been for a long time. You often forget where a player's journey begins, but Melky was a top 10 draft pick, in my draft year. Tom Scully was 1, Jack Trengove was 2, and Jake Melksham was 10. He was best on ground in the TAC Cup Grand Final, and the AFL's national talent manager, Kevin Sheehan, likened him to Saints legend Lenny Hayes. My career started slowly, but it was the opposite for him. Melky developed really quickly as an antagonistic but highly skilled midfielder.

When he came to us, though, he was remade into a forward, which I think was a masterstroke from Goody. He has tricks, and strength, and aggression, and can play tall or small, and gives our attack a hard edge. In 2018 he kicked 32 goals. In 2019 he was largely sidelined by a foot injury. In 2020 he was able to showcase his leadership. In fact, in Round 11 that year I was injured and so was Jack Viney, so Melky stood in as skipper.

Back to misjudging him, Melky is literally *nothing* like the fiery guy you see on the field. He's actually the life of the party – the personality of the group, and at the heart of our sense of humour. He's the guy who sits there on any night out, holding court in the corner, telling jokes and bringing people together. He has three kids – Frankie, Teddy and Alfie – and they're all part of the club, too. He's the perfect example of why you shouldn't judge a book by its cover.

Melky kicked three goals for us against Hawthorn this round – one of them a beautiful left-foot snap in the opening quarter, and the other two as part of that final-quarter avalanche. He's an important part of this machine we've built. He was as close to selection as any of the players who missed out on the Grand Final, too. If Port Adelaide had beaten the Western Bulldogs, for instance, Melky probably would have played, as the perfect defensive forward match up for an interceptor like Aliir Aliir. Sitting in the stands makes for a sad story, but his story isn't over yet. He could have gone looking for a trade to another club, to take his chances elsewhere next season, but he's decided to stay a Demon, to back himself in for another shot at a flag.

I'd love to see him get one alongside Hibbo. Immediately after winning the flag, Hibbo actually said he was doing it for all 34 of the 'Banned Bombers'. Hibbo and Melky are best friends. In fact, that connection is how we ended up with Hibbo. He was thinking about leaving Essendon, and Melky got in his ear – 'Come to Melbourne mate, it's pretty cool here' – and bang, Michael Hibberd arrives at our club at the end of his suspension, and begins playing for us in 2017.

Hibbo found himself out of the team this year, which would have been challenging for him. I have to admit I always thought that once he was out of the team, he might struggle playing at VFL level. It sounds counterintuitive, but there are certain players who shine at AFL level yet struggle when they're playing a rung down. Perhaps they're suited to the pace of the game at the higher echelon. Perhaps it's harder to motivate yourself when you're playing on a scratchy surface in suburban Melbourne in front of a few hundred fans. But I was wrong. Hibbo fought like hell in the VFL, which makes perfect sense – that's where he was originally drafted from.

He has probably the biggest will to win of any player at the club. He just does not want his opponent to get a goal, or even a touch. Having someone like that in your backline is such an asset. Whatever he lacks in physical attributes that someone else in his position might have – like the athleticism of a Joel Smith or the aerobic capacity and height of an Adam Tomlinson – Hibbo just makes up for with pure determination.

This game against Hawthorn was his return to the senior team. He was made to earn his place back, and he did, and the transition was seamless. He gathered 21 disposals, and looked polished and urgent. I remember when the game was in the balance in the third quarter, it was his desperate smother deep in defence that stopped a certain goal, and saw the ball chain out to the other end of the field, ending with a goal to us. That's what he brings – stubbornness and sturdiness, with speed and skill.

He brought that to the team immediately, in fact. In his first year with us, he was named in the All Australian side. Back then, he was a dashing defender off half-back – that player prototype that has pace and delivery and scoring ability. But you know what? I'd rather play with the 2021 Michael Hibberd than the 2017 Michael Hibberd. Something has shifted in him in those years. The new Michael Hibberd just *refuses* to lose a contest. There was a moment in the Grand Final when he was one out with Jason Johannisen, one of the fastest players in the league, and Hibbo clearly decided he simply would not lose that contest. He got it done. It wasn't pretty. It won't make the highlights reel. But those moments mean everything.

And it's hard not to think about who he is as a person when you see those things. Hibbo of course lost his big brother Geoff in 2020. It was in April, and Geoff went missing in a tinny while fishing in Western Port Bay. Everyone was away from the club at the time – in that first long COVID break when the pandemic had only just begun. We couldn't be around him. We couldn't see him. It was so hard, being able only to call or text, and not being able to see him face to face, instead reading his Instagram tribute, which he ended with a plea: 'Hug your loved ones. Tell them you love them. Family is everything.' They were searching for Geoff – his hero – for more than a week.

They still – to this day – have had to reschedule his funeral or wake or party, again and again and again.

It's strange being a club leader in moments like that, navigating tragedies, knowing when to call and what to say and who to lean on. Sometimes you want to do the ego thing – get involved and plot the course – but that's not me. What you actually find when something like that happens is that everyone wants to help, everyone wants to go above and beyond. You'll find a WhatsApp group chat unfolding, or a string of text messages pinging back and forth, dozens and dozens of the things – none directly to the person in trouble, but circling them together, trying to figure out what you can do to help, and how you can put all arms around them. It sounds a strange thing to say, but a football club is a great place to be when something bad happens.

And finally there's Mitchy Brown. He's not connected to the Bomber story in the way that it binds Goody and Melky and Hibbo together but there's a tangent here worth exploring, and in his case it's that familiar story of the long, long road.

Mitch Brown was drafted by Geelong in 2008, and as is the case with so many journeyman footballers, you forget that their careers often started with such burning promise. He was a first-rounder, taken with pick 15, then brought low with bad luck – a broken leg in 2009. In five years with the Cats, he played just 15 games before being delisted.

The supplements saga that became such a setback for Melksham and Hibberd was – perversely – a blessing and a lifeline for Mitch. He was given a short-term contract to play three games for the Bombers in their 2015 pre-season campaign, and then played an entire season of VFL as a swingman for Sandringham. He worked hard and was named centre half-forward in the VFL team of the year, and that earned him an AFL spot again, drafted by Essendon in late 2015, to play there in 2016 as one of the 'top up' Bombers.

It's easy to forget there was an AFL season when James Kelly, Matthew Stokes, Ryan Crowley and Mark Jamar were running around in the red and black. Mitch was there, too. And he did well enough that year that they kept him for 2017. And 2018. And 2019, before he was finally delisted.

Mitch was given the chance to train with us in late 2019. He was given a place on the list in 2020. He got another chance in 2021. He's just signed on for 2022.

I played with Mitch many, many years ago – as a teenager – at the Sandringham Dragons. He was quiet then and he's still quiet now. He's the oldest player on our list, too, but because of that maturity, and because he's been at four clubs (counting the VFL), and because he's played good footy and sometimes thrived, but always survived, people tend to follow him. He does all the right things. He says all the right things. He trains every week. He has kicked bags and bags of goals on Jake Lever at training, which is a wonderful thing. Everybody loves it when Jake gets touched up at training. Mitch has become a great connection between young and old, past and future, AFL and VFL.

Mitch Brown played one senior game for the Melbourne Football Club in 2021, and it was this game in Round 6 against Hawthorn. He more than played his part on the day, and I think that's why he refuses to see himself as a back-up option. He wants to be in the team. He cracks in every week with a place in our best 22 firmly in mind.

He's not content to wait in line. He wants to be ahead of Sam Weideman and Tom McDonald and Ben Brown. And some weeks he will be. Against the Hawks, he took six marks and kicked two goals two behinds. He found his way in, and did what was needed. He knows he can deliver that, and he's not going to let anyone tell him he can't, or won't, or shouldn't at least try.

CHAPTER 7

Round 6

Saturday April 24, 7:25pm
Melbourne Cricket Ground
Melbourne (12.10.82) versus Richmond (6.12.48)

COVID–19 cast a shadow over everything in 2020. And even when the season was long over and we had so many of our freedoms restored, the pandemic was still there, bubbling away, one outbreak or Tier 1 site at a time. Going through pre-season of 2021, and then the early games with crowds, you still felt it – this oozing threat that it would come back.

The states were all doing an enormous job to suppress the coronavirus, and 'COVID zero' was our obsession – *remember that?* Then along came the Delta variant, and things started to change. Outbreaks were harder to contain. Spotfires became wildfires. In the back of your mind you knew at all times that this thing was wildly more infectious than its predecessor. And I remember thinking about the shape of a standard season, and the games we love to play each year, and in my mind I was saying to anyone up there who would listen: Just give us the Anzac Day Eve game. You can take away the crowds after that, but just give us that one game.

And that's what happened – 56,914 people came to the game. That's less than usual, but it was windy and wet and cold, and people were apprehensive about being in a big crowd. It's amazing to play in a truly packed MCG, but this was still special, and I also had to remind myself that for guys like Luke Jackson and Kozzy Pickett and Trent Rivers, this was easily the biggest blockbuster of their careers so far. This was them getting a chance to see big time AFL footy as I've known it for years.

It starts with the build-up. Often we go into the Shrine of Remembrance as a team, in the days approaching the game, mostly to show those younger players what it means to recognise the ANZACs. It's not about *playing* as ANZACs, because we're not that, and we don't try to pretend we are, because that would be an insult to all the people who've risked and lost their lives in honour of something greater. Footy isn't war. You don't want to compare a backline under siege with a unit pinned down in a firefight. But we can still take a moment to study their values, and see where they align with ours.

We couldn't get to the Shrine this year, but we had a guest speaker come to our main training session that week, out at Casey Fields. Mike Oram was his name. Wing Commander Mike Oram of the Royal Australian Air Force – a guy who had flown Black Hawk helicopters in missions over the Sinai Peninsula and Kabul. He came for 30 minutes, and talked to us about the troops who were serving in conflicts around the world at that time, whether Afghanistan or Iraq.

I enjoy that part of this round every year, that we're asking people to consider the battles that are being fought in our name right now, the service that goes beyond the footage we see of the old diggers. I think it's important that our night game appeals to millennials – that we involve them in a modern-day conversation about sacrifice. They're the ones who are going to take these traditions forward.

Wing Commander Oram is a Demons diehard. His wife said that the night before he came to talk to us, he was like a kid on Christmas Eve. He told us how he's watched Melbourne games in the trenches, on his phone, while getting shot at – and this was five years ago, when Melbourne weren't exactly a great side! He talked to us about his kids, who are currently deployed, and he spoke about selflessness, and what it means to put your mates before yourself.

'In my defence force,' he said, 'we don't fight for flags, we don't fight for national anthems or politicians. We fight for our mates. We fight for our families, and for those who are dear to us. We make a commitment to not let each other down, to not let the other bloke carry the load, to put ourselves in harm's way so that others don't have to. Watching the way you guys are playing this year, it's clear that you guys have made this commitment to each other as well. As a fan, it just makes me proud as hell. You're playing for each other, playing for the jumper, and you make every Demon's supporter proud.'

It's hard not to get inspired when someone delivers a message like that. And then there's the night itself. My family treats the Anzac Eve game as a big event, getting there an hour before the bell, and it's easy to see why. It can be breathtaking in that darkened stadium, phones twinkling, Lighthorse marching, cauldron lit, the 'Last Post', the Australian anthem and the New Zealand anthem. I have New Zealand heritage, so I sang the New Zealand anthem. Belted it out. I looked over to see if Dusty Martin was as well, but he wasn't.

In the minute's silence, you think about some of the values you've dwelled on during the week, or you can take the footy option and think about the game itself. But it's hard to turn off completely. There's a hot team immediately across from you, and it's quiet, and then you're into the songs and the warm-up, and the first bounce comes at you quickly.

Richmond certainly needed to win. They were 2 and 3, and would have been desperate to stamp some authority and show their brand. For us, there were still these doubtful whispers about Melbourne, and they wouldn't go away: 'Yeah, they look good, but who have they beaten?' Beating Geelong didn't dispel the naysayers, either. People had noted how Geelong started the year slowly – they weren't yet into that mid-season Cats rampage of 12 straight wins. Yep, going up against the Tigers, the message was clear: 'You haven't knocked over anyone yet. Prove us wrong.'

And in that first 10 minutes of the game, you understood. Everything was just so *hot*. The pressure was immense. The ball was stuck in their forward line and just would not come out. Tomlinson had a handful of massive contests against Jack Reiwoldt, who jagged a soccer goal with his best Lionel Messi impersonation. We just couldn't get it going our way. I remember switching in the ruck with Jacko early, because I wasn't getting it done either and thought maybe his fresh legs would get us going.

It became a really important moment in the context of our season. We actually referred to the first 10 minutes against Richmond for the rest of the year. About how to compose yourself at the start of a game against a team that starts so hot. About how to react when you get hit hard in that first 10 minutes and can't seem to unleash a punch of your own. About how to compose yourself within that storm. About how to keep your cool ... 'like in the Richmond game'.

Because here's the thing – they didn't put that much scoreboard pressure on us. We held up well in defence – and that was the most important point. When a team throws the first punch like that, and then the next, and they're swinging and thrashing, you need to withstand some of it – most of it, all of it – and then go the other way. And eventually, after weathering what they had, we were able to wear them down and push back.

Petracca had 38 touches, including 10 clearances, and kicked the sealer. Oliver had 36, and Langdon 32. McDonald kicked three goals to continue his bright start to the year, while Jackson and Fritsch and Neal-Bullen had a pair of majors each. After fighting his way back into the side a week earlier, Hibbo was enormous.

I remember, the week before, we were all murmuring a little that he was coming back just in time to get ready and primed to take on Dusty Martin. He's tagged Dusty before and done a good job. Once he did so well that it almost looked as though Hibbo was going to be a full-time midfielder for us, doing that run-with role on a regular basis. Dusty was playing more forward this year, too, so it became an even more logical tag for a defender like

Hibbo. Dusty was concussed and subbed out of the game halfway through the third quarter, but he had only had eight possessions when that happened, an amazingly low number for that kind of player. Hibbo did really well.

If Hibbo is someone you think of when you think of desperate footy, there's another guy who plays with a similar sort of rare intensity. The phrase 'white-line fever' gets thrown around often, but one player it certainly applies to is Christian Salem. He is very introverted. Quite timid off the field. Loves his family. He lived at home until last year, when he was 24 years old. But the moment he crosses that white line, he has this aggression at the contest that is unwavering.

I get that his left foot works well, and that he's got a good eye, and that most people might see him as a dashing half-back and creative ball user, but his contest work is almost better. His ability to crack in when it's his turn to go is what always stands out for me. Christian's role changes all the time, too, depending on the balance in the backline and the match-ups we have. When Jayden Hunt is in the team, he's a little better closer to goal, so Christian would play higher. When Jake Bowey came into the team later in the year, he went a bit deeper. Things get juggled around depending on all sorts of factors, and Christian can just adapt to those different roles at the drop of a hat. Looking in from the outside, you might think defence is defence, but there's a complexity to the job. There's six different interlocking parts in our backline, and he can play most of them.

Against Richmond, he played high. Richmond play an extra man at stoppages, so we wanted to utilise our strength – which is having an extra defender running off half-back – and that's what Christian did. Boy did he do it well – 39 touches for the night, for 786 metres gained. It was a breakout game, to the point that when the announcer came to award best on ground – the inaugural Frank 'Checker' Hughes medal – we all heard the word 'Christian' come out of the announcer's mouth and immediately thought she was going to say Salem, not Petracca. We literally thought she had made a mistake – and I'm still not convinced that she didn't! Trac was amazing, but there was something special about Salem's game.

In some ways I guess that suits him fine. As I said, he's not boisterous or flashy, and his story isn't as well worn as some others in the team. He was in the 40-man squad for the All Australian team this year, but didn't make the side. I don't think he's ever been in the top five of our best and fairest, either. But he's going to get his rewards in the coming years. He had only just inked a five-year extension when he played against Richmond, making him an integral part of this new era we're all building.

The story of the Anzac Day Eve game of course can't be told without mentioning Nathan Jones. It was his 300th game – when he became only the second Demon to reach that milestone, after David Neitz (306). I want to talk about what Nathan Jones means to me on a deeper level later, but it's important to recognise this achievement. It's rare air, occupied only by those who extract everything possible out of themselves. To make it to 300 – especially when your team hasn't had the advantage of playing finals every year – is the mark of the ultimate self-made career, and it's something to be celebrated.

It was Angus Brayshaw's 100th game as well, and he tried to call the clash the 'Gunk 400' – a combination of 100 games by 'Gus' and 300 by 'Chunk' – but it didn't really catch on. At all. Milestones are meant to be fun, too, and clubs understand their worth. They helped celebrate all week. They commissioned stories and clips of vision. They called for video tributes sent in from loved ones. The whole week became about Jonesy, and the build-up was intense, as it should be for a warrior of our club.

It was just so exciting to get out there and play with a bit of the Jones spirit. We wanted to play a great Anzac Eve game. We wanted to beat Richmond. We wanted 6 and 0. We wanted it for Jonesy. There was a lot going on. And I could only imagine at the time that *this* is what a grand final would be like in Melbourne. A lot to play for, a lot going on, people coming up to you and sending messages. We almost had a right to be a bit spent or fatigued by the time we started the game.

But we weren't. We got it done, and that moment after the final siren, chairing Jonesy off, knowing we had done it on the big stage for the first time in 18 months, winning a blockbuster game, the Tigers staying to cheer him off – it felt like everything came together. A big crowd and big match, with a big milestone for a big leader – that was just such a high. Such a high.

We didn't know it yet, but we wouldn't see another crowd that size until the finals. It didn't matter. We were undefeated after six rounds for the first time since 1965, and I think that's when many of us first started considering that – maybe, possibly, potentially – this year could be our year. We knew if we kept doing what we were doing, and buying into what we had planned, that 2021 could be something special – a season to remember.

CHAPTER 8
Round 7

Sunday May 2, 1:10pm

Blundstone Arena, Hobart

North Melbourne (11.7.73) versus Melbourne (16.7.103)

The day before we played North Melbourne in Tasmania, I went to the footy. Not to the Pies–Suns game at the MCG or the Saints–Hawks clash at Marvel – I went to see some local footy. I love local footy. I've got mates who play in teams all over Melbourne. When the Demons have a Sunday game or a Friday night game, it's the perfect opportunity to pop down and see some suburban action on a Saturday afternoon.

Living on the Mornington Peninsula, I went really local this time, heading down the road a few minutes to watch Mount Eliza against Sorrento – the Redlegs against the Sharks. Mount Eliza won with the last play of the game, and the fans stormed the oval, and it made the newspaper the next day: 'Fans – *including players from the Melbourne Football Club such as Max Gawn* – stormed the field.' I didn't storm the field, but I was definitely there. I love that atmosphere.

When I was 17 and football was starting to get serious for me, one of the best things about the game was being at some local ground or another and feeling the crowd – no big grandstands, but people lining the oval, or sitting in the front seat of their car watching through the windscreen, honking for goals. The acoustics are completely different. You can hear the spectators and know that most of them are family and friends, or players from other age groups, and you listen to them roaring and your own teammates screaming, and it sort of echoes through the streets of whatever neighbourhood is nearby, and you know you're all in it together. You feel like you're all part of the same battle.

Grassroots footy is where I come from. Commentators love to tell you what private school every AFL player comes from, because the scholarship system is the primary pathway. But I didn't go to one of those big APS/AGS schools – I grew up in McKinnon and was an Ormond footy club boy. I get back to Ormond as much as I can, and will definitely be involved in local footy when my professional career is over. Go the Monders. Up the brown and blue.

A day at an amateur game on the foreshore was meant to be a nice, relaxing start to my working weekend, and it was at first. But things began to get hectic really quickly. COVID outbreaks seemed to be kicking off around the country, and we had to go into isolation that night. It was an odd timeslot, too – a 1.10 pm game on Sunday, but instead of flying into Tassie the night before, we were flying in early Sunday morning.

Usually we fly interstate the day prior, head to the ground for an easy stretch and the captain's run training session, then we go to our hotel, have a meal and meetings, rest up, get up, get to the ground and go. But when you fly in on the same day as the game, *nothing* is relaxed.

We had to be in Launceston by 10 am. That meant I had to wake up at 5 am. But sometimes I beat my alarm clock, and I did this time. I got up thinking I'd had enough sleep. I thought I saw some light shining through the blinds, so I came out into the living area, turned the coffee machine on, fed Charlie – my border collie – and looked at the clock. It was only 1 am. If I had drank the coffee, I would have been cooked, but I was able to pour it out and go right back to bed. Charlie got a surprise midnight snack, and I struggled to get back to sleep.

When I got up for good, I drove down the road to Jake Lever's house, and we drove to the airport together in darkness. The flight was a little delayed, which is always frustrating when you're already sacrificing sleep. We travelled with our opponents, North Melbourne, which is always strange. It would have been stranger for Ben Brown. This was his debut for the Demons, against his old club, in his home state.

I remember his jumper presentation in the rooms. That was a really nice moment. Colin Garland – a fellow Taswegian who played 141 games for us – presented Ben with his guernsey. These presentations are just one small part of extending that invitation to past players to maintain and deepen their connection with the club. These ceremonies can be really meaningful, too. In Round 1, James McDonald presented James Jordan with his jumper. 'Junior' had been our captain – a guy who was recruited as a rookie from the Victorian Amateur Football Association, and who played 251 games with us, winning two best and fairests and All Australian honours. He was a Melbourne champion, and some thought his departure from the club in 2010 wasn't handled as well as it should have been.

We didn't know what to expect from Colin when he presented number 50 to Ben. No-one has worn number 50 at the club, so in a sense Ben was about to start making his own history. Colin's speech reflected that, talking about the hard way Ben had done it, his journey to 'the mainland' to play at the highest level, the way he lobbed in Victoria with the aim of getting a game at Werribee, and how he did that and excelled, and how North Melbourne gave him a chance, and how he repaid that faith. In three seasons, Ben Brown made the All Australian squad but never quite the final team. In 2017, 2018 and 2019 he finished third, second and second in the Coleman Medal, kicking 188 goals over 66 games – more than anyone else in the competition over that time. But then all of a sudden he was on the outer, looking for a new home, and then he was with us at Melbourne. He started slowly, but found form, and now found himself in the senior side, back on the island state. He's an amazing story. He kicked two goals that day against his old side.

As for me, my body felt horrible after that early start, the two-hour-plus drive from Launceston to Hobart and the drawn-out preparation. I played a terrible game. A few of the other older players did, too.

North was never going to be easy to beat down there. There was a stretch recently where the Kangaroos beat us 17 games in a row – one of the longest winning streaks of the modern era – and we've had so many close games against them, too. In 2016 there was the infamous 136 to 131 game. The wind was howling to one end, so North started with a 50 to 14 first quarter, but after taking turns kicking with the gale force breeze, by half-time we were somehow in front. Todd Goldstein kicked five goals, and

I kicked two myself. Boomer Harvey ran riot with six. We lost by five points.

In 2017 we lost again by one kick. In 2018 we beat them, and that was the end of the streak. In 2019 Alex Neal-Bullen had a chance to win the game – he was running into goal from 40 metres and missed as the siren went. That was Jordan Lewis's last game. We've just had crazy battles, and it looked like it was going that way again.

They were a young side, but in front by 19 points at half-time and completely on top of us. We got over the line in the end for a 30-point win, but the game was far closer than that margin might suggest. We got a few goals late, but they had made it hard for us all day. I remember Ben Cunnington was just massive in their midfield. He was just so big and so strong over the ball – we couldn't get it done against him that afternoon. But we had Luke Jackson save us, with 22 possessions and a Rising Star nomination. Bayley Fritsch saved us with six goals. Kozzy Pickett saved us with three goals. Christian Salem and Clayton Oliver saved us with good ball use all game. But the story that day was Adam Tomlinson.

Tommo was one of the inaugural GWS Giants, a guy taken with pick 9 in the 2011 draft, a tall swingman who was said to have the running capacity of Nick Riewoldt. We brought him to Melbourne as a free agent at the end of 2019, and he stepped onto the field for us as that crucial third tall defender in 2020. He really grew into his role in 2021, holding down a dangerous key forward every week, and then his importance really grew in Round 4 against Geelong. Steven May copped an accidental elbow to the face from Tom Hawkins, and his eye socket was fractured, out for a month. Tommo had to step up and take the most potent forward threat every week, and that's exactly what he was doing in Tasmania.

I didn't see what happened to him. I don't remember any commotion. I just remember that Nathan Jones was our medical sub, and then all of a sudden I saw him on the field at a centre bounce and wondered why: 'What are you doing here?'

All he said was 'Tommo', and I assumed that meant a tweaked Achilles or calf. Tommo is an endurance machine, and has had issues with his lower legs. In time you get to know the bodily complaints of every player on the list, particularly if you've just spent an entire summer with that guy, running together in the heat around sandbelt ovals.

I hoped he was all right, then came to the bench and saw that he wasn't. Adam wears his emotions on his sleeve, and had tears under his eyes. I did, too, that day, shedding a few of my own on the bench in the middle of the first quarter. We both knew his knee was cooked, and it's a long journey back from any knee reconstruction. But it must feel even longer when your team is six wins into a season, and starting to believe, because no matter where the season goes you know you're going to miss out on some great stories. I think he knew – immediately – that he was going to miss out on finals.

I have some experience in this area, of course. I've twice done my knee. In 2009 a knee injury wiped out my entire top-age draft year. Then in my second year at Melbourne, in pre-season, I did my knee again. I think I was lucky to suffer that kind of injury at the start of my career. I think it helped me grow up and become an adult pretty quickly. It makes you develop strong habits and a little maturity and resilience. I always say I'm happy, too, that I did them in the off-season or pre-season. That gives you this chance to wipe out a year, but heal and grow strong before starting a new pre-season fresh.

That helps me relate to someone like Aaron Nietschke, who's young but has done three knees in three years. For him to keep coming back and doing the weights and joining in all the meetings and being a contributor, knowing he was probably not going to be here next year, it was a testament to his character – as a good strong farmer from South Australia.

I can also relate to a guy like Marty Hore – a young guy on the fringe, waiting and waiting for his opportunity – but who hasn't played a game in two years because of injury. Marty missed most of 2020 after tearing his quad from the bone, and then he ruptured his ACL at training on a Friday morning in January. That kind of setback and heartbreak is familiar to me.

I worry more about older guys who do a knee halfway through the year, and have to try to get back into football when they'll only get a limited pre-season. I worry when it's a guy like Tommo, who's now 28, and has seen an opportunity for a premiership medal slip through his fingers. He's done well since then, learning how to coach and remaining a positive presence and great mate. He's almost become the driving force for a flag next year, along with someone like Jayden Hunt, who played 20 games this season but missed out on the game that counted most, or a guy like Sam Weideman, who was in and out of the side and would have had suitors elsewhere but is backing his ability to win a place in the 22. Or Kade Chandler, who was firing at the next level and waiting for his shot, and was an emergency for the Grand Final. Those guys will all be back. Tommo will be back, too. He's in full training already, and he'll be ready to go in Round 1, 2022. He's lucky in that sense, but no-one wants to be lucky in that sense.

As for the match itself, this felt like a game that the old Melbourne might have lost. Trailing in cold, blustery conditions, we could have found ourselves in one of those games where we would fall back into old habits, waiting for one or two or three of us to strap on the capes and try to save the game through stardom. But this was a collective effort, and it felt emblematic of something new. It was gritty and emotional. The game has almost been erased from my memory, because it was so tiring and taxing. We didn't get home until about 10.30 that night, then I complained all week that you should never have to fly interstate on the morning of a game that starts so early in the afternoon. We had won, but Tommo was suffering and I was sour on everything. Just grumpy at the world. Angry all week. Winning isn't always good fun.

CHAPTER 9

Round 8

Saturday May 8, 7:25pm

Melbourne Cricket Ground

Melbourne (10.7.67) versus Sydney (8.10.58)

The Demons versus the Swans might seem like one of those games that will simply fade from memory, but it actually became another of those contests we referred to all season long. It was a tight and dogged game, which was unexpected given how freely Sydney had been moving the ball in the early stages of the year. What stood out immediately on the night, and in the review afterwards, was us not being able to get the ball out of our defensive 50, and just continually inviting pressure on ourselves.

If that doesn't sound particularly relevant, consider the third quarter of the Grand Final, and the way the Bulldogs locked the ball deep in their forward half, troubling and harassing our defenders. The Swans tried to do that to us all night at the MCG, and we felt it, and we learned lessons about how we structure up, how our midfielders position themselves, when to blast with handball and when to bail out with a quick dump kick. You can learn what will work by fully understanding what won't.

I remember that Steven May did a great job on Lance Franklin, keeping him almost statless. He's really good at setting himself a task on a champion, someone he respects. Shutting down Buddy is all he would have thought about all week. He was on. It felt like Sydney outplayed us that night, but guys like May kept us well and truly in the contest.

I had a good battle with Tom Hickey, who was probably the competition's in-form ruckman throughout the start of the year. He kicked a little rover's goal on me early – I was nowhere near him, but he was still my man. I think I was still feeling the effects of the North Melbourne game a week earlier. I couldn't shake how sluggish I felt, and how frustrated, and now I was playing more sluggish footy against a frustratingly energetic opponent. That game was tough for me – I felt genuinely out of form. Sometimes that happens. You aren't reading the play well. You're not on your toes anticipating the things you should. I felt unfit. I felt unwell. I lacked energy. But we were able to win, and I was happy about that, and I was also happy that our forward line finally seemed to be functioning.

In many ways, the story of the match was the cohesion of Tom McDonald and Ben Brown, our twin towers firing together as one. McDonald had 18 touches and four goals. Brown had six marks and three goals. They combined for seven majors on a night the entire team kicked only 10. That would have seemed so unlikely at the tail end of last season, especially for Tom McDonald. In the 2020 trade period, he was encouraged to look at other clubs, and see if it might suit him to move on, a full decade after being drafted by Melbourne in 2010.

I arrived at the club only a season earlier than Tommy, but his journey since then is different to mine. I was in and out of the side when we were losing, whereas Tommy was a mainstay. He was instantly plugged into a key defensive post, and he played with passion and athleticism. He was getting rewarded with best and fairest votes, and came third one year, whereas I was 'the problem guy', the one who was dropped every second week. He jokes that he was getting best on ground because his opponent had kicked only five goals. You had to find a way to smile in those days. He still remembers how hard it got, like the time we won just two games for the year, and players were getting spat on in the race on the way off the field. But that early era also forged him into a player. He and James Frawley and Lynden Dunn created this backline bond, built on shared strength and heart.

His shift to the forward line didn't come until 2017. We needed a second ruck, and there was a game against the Adelaide Crows when we needed to move him around. I was injured, and Cam Pedersen and Jack Watts were really makeshift rucks, yet Tommy looked like a genuine forward-ruck option. He went from being a defender who had played his first 59 games without a single goal, to a forward who kicked 23 goals that season – and 53 goals the following season. He started by coming in and playing a ripping half in the ruck against Sam 'Sauce' Jacobs, and then a dynamic two quarters in the forward line, and it was, like, he is *never* going to be a backman again.

But it's funny, because that was four years ago now, and Simon Goodwin *still* gets asked in press conferences whether Tommy will go back to defence. It happens every time our stock of tall forwards looks deep and threatening, and every time one of our key defenders goes down with injury. And every single time, Goody simply has to play the same straight bat back at reporters: 'No, Tom McDonald will not be going back to defence.' Funnily enough, it could easily have gone that way for the Grand Final. If that hamstring injury to Steven May had kept him from playing.

Tommy was injured for much of 2019, and then even more in 2020, and that would have been hard. Harder still was being told to go and try to find another club, if he could. Sometimes that move is best for both club and player, as a chance to change and reinvigorate, but it would still sting. If there had been a suitor, Tommy would have left, but there wasn't, and that in itself must be a humbling experience. He had every right to get his back up, and return to training a bit prickly. Tommy is normally our best time trial runner – this time he came back even fitter. He got himself a personal trainer and shed kilos. He was so fit he looked like he could play midfield if needed.

His temperament suited the moment. Some players hear all the noise – all that critical static that buzzes around in footy media – but he doesn't listen to it, doesn't watch it, doesn't read it. Nothing gets in. And it's not as if he isn't intimately connected to the wider football world. He's the AFL Players Association representative at the club, a staunch union man. He loves helping out young players, making sure they study, and he does too, chipping away at a course in business.

I wish he could study meat. He loves meat. At the start of this year, when he knew he had to get fitter, he threw himself into a new fitness program – but he also decided to go on an all-meat diet. He was a big meat guy already, but this is just next level. He's started a group at Melbourne called 'Meat Club'. In the hub this year, he brought his own barbecue, and we would all sit around having these marbled M9 grade – that's top of the scale – Wagyu steaks.

They melt in your mouth. I almost can't go back to a regular scotch fillet. And Tommy can cook it 10 different ways. In his backyard he's got the smoker, the barbecue, the grill – he's a fascinating person, and probably the weirdest guy I've met in football. A lot of people who are weird have a normal switch, but he *can't* switch to normal. Tom McDonald just stays at Tom McDonald. He is his own person.

It's great to go immediately from Tom McDonald to Ben Brown, because Ben is a vegan. Two different tall forwards with two different food preferences, but both performing to the same high level, which perhaps goes to show that diet doesn't matter as long as you're keeping away from the bad stuff.

Ben has a bit in common with Tom in that he is his own person, too, and won't be someone else to please anybody. He doesn't try to conform, and that was apparent from day one at the club, and that takes some inner strength. Settling into a new environment, trying to make new friends, you can easily edit yourself for others – trying to meld yourself into the stereotype people expect, or the individual you think people want you to be – but he remained Ben Brown. And he stands up for what he thinks is right, which is a great quality to have.

He's a family man, and I know we say that about people often, but it does run deeper for some than others. It was an incredibly difficult decision for Ben to leave his family and head to Perth for the finals series.

We had to have those conversations with all the players who are dads, because no families were allowed to travel to Perth, and Ben has two very young ones at home. He wasn't the only one to be put under that stress, but I know he felt it acutely. People might think that's an easy decision – to be gone for a month for a crack at a flag – but remember this was a tough month in another long Victorian lockdown. No-one has the right – or the knowledge – to judge anyone else's personal circumstances.

I was really impressed with the way Ben carried himself all year long. He just turned from what we saw in pre-season – someone who had been injured in the past and who hadn't trained much over the past three years – to someone who would not stop training. He was still behind other players at the beginning of the year, and he missed Round 1, and he got a minor injury, then he battled Sam Weideman to win his place in the side, got a few games, and got dropped.

I remember watching him one day after he went back to the VFL, and he was kept completely in check by his less-credentialled opponent. People later asked me, 'How did Brown go?' and all I could say was that *Mitch* Brown had kicked six goals – because poor old *Ben* Brown got maybe two handballs. That game became a turning point for Ben, and his standards just surged. He fought his way back into the side, and he became the focal point of our forward line.

The important thing about Ben is his ability to launch at the footy, running and jumping and fighting to get his hands up in the air, and that's exactly how he gets marks and free kicks – and also how he provides crumbs for our small forwards. He's hard to play against, and he creates goals for others.

Commentator (and AFLW Melbourne captain) Daisy Pearce pointed out a statistic early in the finals that showed the stark value of having Ben in the side. At that point he had played 12 games for the year, and two of our most dangerous small forwards – Kozzy Pickett and Charlie Spargo – had both played 24. So there was this perfect means of measuring Ben's value to the forward line. All you had to do was compare the output of Kozzy and Spargs in the 12 games Ben was there, and the 12 games he wasn't. When Ben was there, Kozzy and Spargs combined for 35 goals. When he wasn't, they kicked 22. That's significant. Tom McDonald is a part of that, too, of course, as is Luke Jackson, flying for his own grabs in that same space.

The game against Sydney was pivotal to the season. A dour match, in which we were challenged – in front by only four points early in the final quarter – and our big boys finally clicked together. They carried the scoreline that night, Tommy using his tank to roam up the field, and Ben streaming out of the goal square looking to grab the ball at its highest point. Sam Weideman was tearing it up in the VFL, too, kicking 14 goals in three games, so it was always going to take something special to keep him out of the side. A pivotal pairing in a seesawing match with a close finish did the trick.

CHAPTER 10

Round 9

Sunday May 16, 3:20pm

Melbourne Cricket Ground

Melbourne (13.16.94) versus Carlton (10.8.68)

I'll tell you a short story about the start of our Round 9 game against Carlton. The Blues have this young midfielder named Sam Walsh. James Harmes played on Walsh in the first quarter, applying a nice, tight run-with role. That's one of his specialties, making an opponent miserable. I was trying to help Harmesy by getting stuck into Walsh a little, too: 'Your game is *nowhere*, mate!' He was only 20 years old, copping a verbal barrage from me, getting tagged by our toughest midfielder, and probably getting bashed into by Christian Petracca every time he ran past. Then I looked at the quarter-time stats, and Sam Walsh's numbers were superb. He must have had 10 touches already. I remember Harmesy coming into the huddle and saying, 'That is the hardest player … I have *ever* played on. He just runs, runs, runs. I am completely rooted.' We had to stop the tag. So, for what it's worth, Sam Walsh is going to be a star, if he isn't already.

For us, I noticed a guy who continued to emerge this season – quietly but steadily – in James Jordon. James was drafted by the club with pick 33 in 2018, but he had to wait until the start of this year for his debut. It's funny how that happens for some players. It can come down to their own physical readiness, or understanding of the game plan, or trouble with injury, or the needs of the team at a particular time, or just the preference of the coach in the moment – but some guys play immediately while others are forced to wait two-and-a-half years for a taste of senior footy. James had to wait, and so he made it count.

He was huge against Sydney the week before, with 23 touches and eight tackles, and it won him a Rising Star nomination. Then he backed it up against the Blues with 20 touches and a whopping 13 tackles. And I think we all just started to realise how important he was to our team. Guys who were out of the team – like Aaron vandenBerg and Nathan Jones and Kade Chandler, who weren't getting a game – were starting to realise why this guy was playing in front of them. He was putting together some really reliable and consistent football, and sometimes, in some roles, that's more important than starring. Being dependable has value. It counts if you can be counted upon.

James ended up playing all 25 games for us in 2021, but it wouldn't have felt easy or stable or secure. He had a constant running battle with Tom Sparrow, for instance, where one would play and the other would be the medical sub, and vice-versa, back and forth, all year long. Sparrow eventually won that and landed on the field, while James was the medical sub for all three finals.

It's hard to know exactly how James feels about that part. He knows he was part of the team. He knows he made the Grand Final side where a host of others didn't. We had some pretty big pushes internally for Jones and Melksham and Hunt to get into the team late in the season, but the selection committee stayed with Jordon as the sub. The debates were strong. I don't look at him as the Grand Final sub, by the way. I look at him as part of the Grand Final team, every bit as deserving of his medal as anyone else. The AFL saw us as a squad of 23. Match committee saw us as a squad of 23. And we all saw ourselves as a squad of 23. But perhaps getting into the 22 is what will drive him next year.

That might be his new individual motivation, but he's also as selfless as players come. The role he plays – and this is the same for Tom Sparrow – means they really only spend 65 per cent of the game on the field. They play a high half-forward role, and maybe they cover for Angus Brayshaw on the wing when he needs a rest, and maybe they go to two or three centre bounces when Petracca or Oliver need to come off. They do this so that we can give other players a rest, but it means that James and Tom often sit on the bench for the other half of the game, and if the team plays poorly and has a loss, they're often the first one dropped. That must be hard to get your head around, and making it even harder is the fact that it's one of our most competitive positions, with at least three more guys waiting in the wings to fill that slot.

We talk about footy sides as being 45 mates all working toward a singular cause, but there's a lot of competition, too. It's natural. In the daily 9 to 5 at the club, you don't really see people wearing it in their mood. But let's say it's early days in my career, and I'm in the VFL, and I'm driving home, and I make a phone call to Mum and Dad. I'm out of the team to Mark Jamar, and Dad might say, 'Mark Jamar didn't play that well this week', and you think to yourself, 'Yeah, he was a little quiet'. And that's often how it happens – your family brings it up, or your friends bring it up, or if you're reading external media then they bring it up, so then it seeps into your head. But when you come into the club you have to shut that out. Because in the end, you'll get picked based on your merit, not on how the competitor for your spot is going.

But those small rivalries do linger, and they drive the healthiest form of competition. You could see that all pre-season long this year. We do a lot of competitive simulation, and we often divide up into opposing sides, red and blue. The blue mids are usually our A grade midfielders, and I remember that they didn't win a midfield battle for the first five weeks of summer. Jordon, Sparrow, vandenBerg and Jones were just *smashing* Oliver, Petracca, Viney and Harmes. And that put us in a really good space.

I know about this stuff all too well, because the ruck battle is the biggest one, as there's literally only one spot for a ruck on the field. When I got drafted, there were six rucks on our list. We were so well supplied with ruckmen that I ended up playing not just VFL but VFL reserves. Now it's really only myself and Majak Daw, and I feel bad for Maj because he's just played one of the best VFL seasons you could, but because I was never injured he just didn't get a look in at senior level. But as I said, I've been there, I know what it's like, and that's just the way some positions work. It's why so many ruckmen change clubs every year during the trade period. There can be only one.

To each player on the fringe, the emotions would be nearly identical. Take a guy like Jayden Hunt. If he was speaking to his family in the approach to the Grand Final, they would have been saying to him, 'I can see a way for you to get into that team – hopefully the coaches will see that Jake Bowey is too young for such a big game, or maybe they'll want Michael Hibberd to play a tagging role on Jack Macrae, and you'll be needed on a back flank', and it takes a really strong person to just shut all of that out. You can dump your hurt feelings with them, if it helps. And you can dump to your manager, too – they'll listen. But in the end the only person who's going to change it is you. Staying focused and remaining hopeful is all you can do. And Hunty did. He didn't show that he was in a rivalry with anyone. He just wanted to play.

He wasn't alone. There were hard luck stories everywhere. Kade Chandler is the next best small forward in the side, and was playing unbelievable footy in the VFL – but Kozzy, Spargs and 'Nibbler' (Neal-Bullen) didn't get injured. They played practically every single game. Kade played against the Blues, but he was out of the team the following week, and then he just had to wait. And sometimes there's nothing at the end of that wait.

A final important part in our Round 9 performance was the showing of a guy named Ed Langdon. Sam Walsh is a jet, and he can run, but I doubt he can run as long or hard as Ed Langdon. Ed's the king of his wing. Most players – particularly running midfielders – need time on the bench to rest, to suck in the air and go again. But Ed can stay out on the field so much longer than most. He showed us that last season, after coming to us from Fremantle, and he started that way again this season, too. I think 2021, with the return to longer, 20-minute quarters plus time-on and a cap on rotations, was always going to favour his endurance. And looking at his stats for time on ground, it really did. In Round 1 he spent 94 per cent of the game on the field, and in Round 2 he was out there 100 per cent of the match – he just never came off.

Now, Ed *wants* to play every minute of the game. Most players do. But most players don't have that capacity. And what Ed's capacity means to us is that Petracca and Oliver and Harmes and Brayshaw can use more of our allotted rotations, to get a better rest, so that when they're back on the ground and in the middle of the action they have maximum reserves of energy to play their brutal power games at stoppages.

It's a cliché to say that a player is 'underrated externally yet valued internally', but it's true of Ed. People who aren't Melbourne supporters might be surprised to learn that he came fourth in our best and fairest in 2020. They might be further surprised to learn that this wasn't enough for him. He wanted desperately to improve.

He gets quite a bit of the footy, for instance. Against GWS, he had 27 touches for 903 metres gained. But he's not really about those numbers anymore.

He talked about this in the off-season, about how the wing had become a bit stale and boring, and how Simon

Goodwin had put something special on his agenda. Goody wanted him to be more attacking, to bring flair and excitement to the side. He wanted him to go away and work on his kicking – especially his goalkicking – and to make it a weapon. He had 24 touches and a goal against the Blues, and in 2021 he kicked 13 goals – the most he has in any year. He grew almost into a target player for other teams to try to shut down.

He wouldn't care about those stats at all though. He just wants success. He might have thought when he switched to us that success had passed him by, because we finished ninth, but he got it, and he's only 25, so he'll be part of a great team for the next few years. He has a real chance to keep striving for success and longevity.

He's a funny guy though. He says he wants to retire at 29 – that he wants to be a man of the world, and be utterly uncontactable, and to travel the globe by himself and be where no-one knows where he is. I wouldn't put it past him, but I wouldn't put my money on it, either. Ed sometimes thinks he's too cool for footy, but I think footy will always get him in the end.

We won the game itself quite comfortably. The Blues started well and had us on the back foot, but we kicked six of seven goals either side of the quarter-time break, giving us a nice three-goal buffer near half-time. From there on, we were able to keep them at arm's length. The rain came down in a torrent at half-time, and with sloppy conditions it became simpler to run out a stress-free victory. That happens sometimes.

It wasn't the most thrilling triumph in football – a sodden twilight game in front of 38,581 fans – but there was something special about it. This was our ninth straight victory. The evidence was building. No Melbourne side had started that well since 1956.

That's the year the Summer Olympics were staged here. It's the year *The Ten Commandments* was the biggest movie in the world. It's the year Dean Martin's 'Memories Are Made of This' was the hit song on radio. It's hard to know what people watched on television, because that's the year television was introduced to Australia.

Something was building, all right. Something was happening. Something else happened in 1956: Melbourne won the flag.

CHAPTER 11

Round 10

Saturday May 22, 4:05pm

Adelaide Oval

Adelaide (15.6.96) versus Melbourne (14.11.95)

I've thought about this a lot, and even said it a few times, so I'll stand by it now. In Round 10 of the 2021 AFL season, in the City of Churches, in a nail-biting loss, I witnessed what I think might be the best individual midfield performance I've ever seen. It came from Clayton Oliver. His statistics say plenty – 38 disposals, 14 clearances, nine tackles and three goals – but if you've ever watched Clayton play, you'll know that there's a freakish quality to those possessions that elevates their value.

His skill set is almost unlike any I've seen. It's about the way he takes possession of the Sherrin, wrenching a bobbling ball from the chaos of a pack. It doesn't matter if the ball is spilling off high grasping hands or if it ricochets off shins at ground level like a pinball, he has this soft touch in the way he receives it into his palms and fingers, like some magnetic pull on the leather itself. He reaches, it sticks, and then he's away.

What I saw from him that night almost single-handedly got us over the line, and that's probably not a surprise to anyone. He finished third in the Brownlow Medal with 31 votes – the most polled by any Melbourne player in history – and has been a star and a stalwart almost since he started playing with us. He's 24, and has also just won two best and fairests in a row.

His only problem until this year was that he didn't kick with penetration or composure. He spoke publicly about this exact issue.

It's not the first time he's improved himself. His fitness was questioned as a draft prospect when he was playing for the Murray Bushrangers. That played a big part in his brilliant second half of the TAC Cup season. He won the VFL Morrish Medal in 2015, after only polling once in the first nine rounds. People sometimes wonder how a special player can emerge out of nowhere late in the year, coming from the clouds to be worthy of an early first-round selection. Clayton Oliver, pick number 4 in 2015, is the very definition of a 'draft bolter'. This time – this year – the carrot was team success.

All he wanted to do at the start of the season was be a better teammate. Everyone has these sheets in their locker, which have messages written on them. It's there so you get this little reminder every time you put your jumper on or take it off. Mine has a few things, like 'Create a great midfield' and 'Be a good ruck'. There's much more to it, and smaller points under each of those headings.

Clayton's just reads, 'Be the best teammate you can be'. Ask the defenders and they'll tell you who gets back to help out as much as possible. Ask the other mids and they'll tell you about the pressure he puts on to release others. Ask the forwards and they'll thank him for the deliveries he's worked so hard on improving.

Clayton has just an extreme will to win – he's our midfielder with that trait. When things get close in a game, and the pressure is mounting and we need a spark, I like to tap the ball to Clayton, because he's the guy for that moment. And it's funny, the instant he set his own personal goal as being the best possible player for the team, he became the best version of himself as an *individual* player. Strange how that works – or maybe it isn't. His three goals that night against Adelaide were incredible – snaps, low drills across the body, from clearances, immaculate, unfathomable. But, of course, they weren't quite enough.

It was a tough game against the Crows. I'm not sure how, but they found a way around our defence. We were a little off, and they pierced us. They scored 96 points – the highest score against us all year.

We almost got over the line. We were in front for most of the game. Big Tex Walker put them in front with not long to play. Then there was an umpiring decision not paid to us in the dying seconds, when the ball was rushed over the boundary line deliberately. That got blown up afterwards, but make no mistake, Adelaide absolutely deserved to win. It was a deflating finish. And sad in more than one way. We didn't know it at the time, but this loss would also be the last game for one of our spiritual leaders – the 159th and final AFL match of Neville Jetta.

Nev was taken in the same draft as Jack Watts, Sam Blease, James Strauss and Jamie Bennell. He was taken after all of them, in fact, with pick 51, but outlasted them all anyway. He struggled at first, playing just 41 games in five years. Paul Roos eventually kept him on the list as a rookie in 2014, and from then on he became an indispensable cog, then a star. People forget that about Nev. Because he started slowly and ended quietly, they forget how good he got in the middle, close to All Australian in both 2017 and 2018. Quiet back pockets don't get much recognition from the wider community, but if you ask guys like Eddie Betts who their toughest opponents were, Nev would be up there. Roosy said if he had to pick a player to play for his very *life*, it would be Nev.

And he was a catalyst for a lot of our early work with Roosy, building this culture, particularly with some of the young Indigenous players. He's gone to Collingwood now in a playing coaching role, and they've got an absolute belter there. He puts everyone before himself. That might have been what got him in the end. Nev was a great teacher-trainer. He trained up all the small forwards to understand how to play against backmen like him. And he trained up the small defenders with fresher legs who've taken his spot. Maybe he could have been more of a rebounder, which is what he trained Trent Rivers and Jake Bowey to be.

One other thing bothers me about his final season, and it's the racial attacks he had to deal with. Neville designed a jumper for his 150th game – a special artwork to honour his family – and bang, Instagram comments appeared. For some players, that kind of unacceptable abuse is part and parcel of their career. But when it pops out, it's baffling. This year in particular we've seen social media get away from us. Nev wasn't the only one. Kozzy Pickett had to deal with it too.

I know that would have hurt Nev just as much as Kozzy. Kozzy is his nephew, after all. They lived together when Kozzy was first drafted. Their connection is strong. When we won the Grand Final, Kozzy tried to give his premiership medal to Nev – he literally tried to put it around his neck. But no way was Nev going to have that. He did grab the premiership cup, though, just for a minute, just as we were about to go back into the rooms. I'm so glad he had that moment.

I want to do better and do more on race and football as the years go by, because I'm tired of seeing this happen to people I love. The first thing you feel when you see it – as a white male – is guilt, because you realise that your type – other white males – are the problem. Guys like Nev and Steven May get tired of being the ones to respond, as if it's their problem, because it's not. We heard Eddie Betts this year saying the same thing: 'I'm tired.' The guys are exhausted, and they need help, especially from high-profile players. I'm ready to step in and fight that battle whenever I can, because you know it won't change until we all step up and hold people accountable.

I've had teammates in the early days – and certainly friends – use the language of casual racism. It's all too common. I've never had to deal with changing the way I speak, because I wasn't raised that way, but for a while I also thought that meant 'This is not my problem'. But it *is* my problem. Just because I've never been casually racist doesn't mean I can escape racism, doesn't mean I don't have to call it out, doesn't mean I never have to step up against it. I have to, because it's the right thing to do, and because I don't want to see anyone else feel that hurt or carry that load, because it's bullshit.

It makes me sad that Nev had to end his career in a year in which that happened, and on a day where we lost by a point. That was the end of the streak, of course. We were 9 and 1 now. But we were also ready for the day when that run came to an end. Goody had prepared us in advance. We had talked in depth about great sporting streaks. There was the recent 28-game unbeaten streak of Premier League soccer team Manchester City. There was the Golden State Warriors streak five years ago in the NBA, which lasted 54 games. And of course there was the famous Major League Baseball streak of the Oakland Athletics' 20-game run, which happened 20 years ago and was immortalised in the book and film *Moneyball*.

The message Goody wanted to share was that you're not really remembered for the streak itself, but for winning on the final day of the season. By all means, he told us, be fascinated by the streak, and happy about it, and want to create something great, but don't put your head into it too deeply, because there's a goal at the end of the season, and it has nothing to do with how many consecutive wins you string together on the way there.

The feeling in the hotel was bad. We were top of the ladder, and the Crows were bottom four. But it also felt like an exciting game. We were in Adelaide for two nights, and the Adelaide Oval crowd was roaring, and just so incredibly loud when Tex kicked his goal in the last minute. Sure the result went against us, but that atmosphere still gets you up. That's why you want to play footy.

I remember in the centre bounce, when we had one last chance to win it – I like to think that most oppositions would expect us to try something special, so I decided to go normal, double-bluff them and play it safe. But Petracca said, 'No, put it out to the right side, 3 o'clock, your off-hand hit, and I'll do the rest.' He gets it there, Kozzy goes for a mark and gets spoiled, which I thought was a free kick. I bolt to get down there for the stoppage. The ball goes out of bounds, no whistle. I try to grab it out of the ruck but their pressure is immense. Siren sounds. Game over. Yeah, we lost, but the crowd was crazy, their superhero kicked the winner, and I saw one of the best midfield performances ever. That's really why you play.

Externally – and this is our fault for the way we've performed over the years – the fans feel like Doomsday has arrived, that all their worst fears have been realised, that the 'same old Melbourne' is back. It's hard for them to shake those feelings with such defeats. People lose heart. Board members, family members, fans – they feel it all.

That's why one of the most important things I have printed on my reminder sheet, in my locker at the club, is this pledge: 'To change how this club has been viewed externally and internally.' I want to break that cycle. I go into every game thinking we're going to win, and it's always been that way for me. We might have been playing injured, away, against the Hawthorn dynasty at their peak, and I'd still be going in thinking, 'We're a chance here.' I want that hope and belief for everyone.

Footy clubs are great places at resetting, analysing, and moving on quickly. And after a loss like that, you have great mechanisms in place. We did our review two days later, but here's the thing about match review: it's the same whether you've won or lost. You don't dissect the game differently on the basis of the result.

Coaches find the clips worth showing no matter what happened on the scoreboard. They find the mistakes and errors of judgement they want to highlight, and play those, noting, 'We don't want this', and they play the positive clips where we made the right choices while noting, 'We do want this'. There's almost always a lot of both to uncover.

And for me, from a leadership perspective, there's just no point in being the frustrated captain, because everyone will see that and it will affect them. After any loss, you have to make sure that when Tuesday comes around you're 'Positive Peggy' from then onwards. You move swiftly on to opposition analysis, and how you think the next game will be played.

In our case, a top-of-the-table clash against the Western Bulldogs was waiting, only six days away. Against that sort of clock you haven't got time to stew over one-point losses – you immediately get your head into 'This is what *we* do' and 'This is what the Doggies will do' – 'Here are our weapons' and 'Here's what they're gonna bring'. Three days after the Round 10 loss, we felt completely and utterly prepared for a Round 11 win. We moved on, set it up, and got back to where we needed to be. We were hot for that game.

CHAPTER 12

Round 11

Friday May 28, 7:50pm
Marvel Stadium
Western Bulldogs (8.11.59) versus Melbourne (13.9.87)

When we got home from Adelaide, it felt as though the season had immediately changed. COVID cases kicked off in Melbourne again, and instantly we were swept up in lockdowns and protocols. We were about to play the Western Bulldogs, and both teams had an unusual build-up. Their team was forced to isolate after a staff member was found to have visited a Tier 1 exposure site, which meant they weren't allowed to do their main training session. Then we had our issue, with an injured player visiting the The Sporting Globe bar in Mordialloc, which also became a Tier 1 site, meaning we couldn't do our captain's run.

To not have a captain's run, and be locked into your house for 24 hours prior to the game, was familiar from

2020, but still strange. I ran on a treadmill in my garage. I know other players ran up and down in their hallway or backyard. You really do want to blow out the cobwebs and get the heart rate up a little before a game. We got a great example of just how far athletes go with that kind of pre-performance warm-up.

Our fitness boss, Darren Burgess, had taken a group of us to the Australian Open in January. We went to watch Rafael Nadal and Novak Djokovic, but not during their match. We went early – around four hours early – to watch them train. Tennis players practise quite hard on the day of their match. It was a scorching Melbourne day, and they were smashing forehands and serves, and running back and forth, up on their toes. It was a proper, full intensity 60-minute workout, and this was the day of a match, both of them knowing that match could turn into some epic five-hour, five-set contest. But they needed the workout to get that little bit of rhythm and looseness into their bodies, and that's what we need, too – a final chance to feel that connection with what a good kick looks like, or how soft hands feel. Burgo makes us get a little speed into our day, too. This time we were doing it at home.

We also had our meeting, and that's the big team meeting of the week, where Goody presents the game, but we had to do it on Zoom, and it was just a nightmare. I remember he threw to Angus Brayshaw early and asked,

'What was our mission statement from the start of the season?' He thought Angus would know, and Angus got it completely wrong, and Goody didn't know what to do, except listen to a few laughs and then explain it himself. There were stops and starts with technical issues, and we were finally starting to get into a groove talking about what the Western Bulldogs do at a defensive stoppage, when Choco Williams turned his mic off mute and blurted out, 'Um, just a quick question: Are we going to be able to do our normal warm-up kick before the game?' He took us completely off topic, and I'm shaking my head, and I can see Goody with his face in his hands, knowing this Zoom presentation has just gone off the rails. But Goody got there in the end, and he set up a demand – asking all the leaders to write private non-negotiables for wearing a Melbourne jumper. These are things that we shared with one another but kept in-house – things that were established then and there, and set for the rest of the year. The meeting format was so artificial, but out of it we got something real.

Everything about the build-up to that game was weird. We hadn't done the full COVID-safe approach to a match in a while, doing a couple of COVID tests in the day prior, getting a work permit to move throughout Melbourne, arriving at a ground knowing that not a single soul would be sitting in the grandstands, and getting out onto the turf for a walk and a stretch wearing facemasks. Marvel

Stadium is an eerie place for that kind of game, too. In the middle of winter – with the closed roof and all that cold concrete – it feels so deserted. We had only played a game without crowds there once, against Carlton the year before. Everything echoes. You notice that immediately out on the ground.

We started electrically well, it began in the centre, where I grabbed the ball out of the ruck, surged it forward, and Sam Weideman made an amazing contest, Clayton Oliver did brilliantly at ground level and the ball squeezed to James Harmes, who kicked a goal. We had a major on the board within 20 seconds, and it felt as though everyone got a lick of the ice-cream. The noise from all the players was just so loud and it carried all around the stadium, and that's exactly how you want to start in that situation. From then on, I only heard *our* noise for the whole game. I couldn't hear the Dogs at all. I could hear Choco on the bench, so loud it was almost funny. There was one Bulldog I did hear: half-back Taylor Duryea actually yelled at Choco at one point to shut the hell up, which was pretty funny, because we could all hear that, too.

Both clubs had entered that contest at 9 and 1. The Bulldogs had played five games at Marvel Stadium – their home ground – and won them all by an average margin of almost 11 goals. They thumped North Melbourne early on by 128 points, and they were in form there, too, having walloped St Kilda by 111 points only a week prior. They run the ball with a kind of rampant abandon – you never know when or where they're going to shuffle that footy with a handball. That's why this game stood out for us all season as one of our best. We won by 28 points.

That game was pure. If you look at our internal KPIs throughout the season, that game comes up as one of our best – maybe the very best – on all measures. We actually did a trivia session in the hub in Western Australia later, and there were three or four footy questions in a row – 'What was our highest contested possession differential game?' or 'What was our best locked in our forward-half game?' – and they all ended up being that Western Bulldogs game in Round 11. It was *exactly* how we wanted to perform – pure Melbourne football. We did have a secret weapon that night: James Harmes playing on Tom Liberatore. The Bulldogs have two of the most damaging and prolific midfielders in the competition in Marcus Bontempelli and Jack Macrae, and throughout the season so far most teams would send a tagger to one of them. Goody decided to go a different way, trying to blunt the impact of Libba instead. When he first said it I thought, 'That's interesting.' I thought Bont would have been the man, a similar target to Dusty Martin, because they both rotate through the forward line. But Libba is that guy who's always in the centre of things for the Bulldogs –

right at the coalface. The thinking was that he was their catalyst – the one who feeds the ball to Bont and Macrae and Hunter and Smith and Dunkley – so maybe we could stop them at the source. I don't think anyone expected we would send Harmes to Libba, but that's where we went, and I think it shows how highly we rate him. I also think it was a coaching masterstroke. And I know it got Harmesy back to being Harmesy.

What can I say about James Harmes? He's an extreme confidence player, and not everyone is. That just means he plays really well when he's feeling good about himself, when he has a role he wants, and when people are clear with him. Recognising that there are guys like that in your team is an important part of leadership, too. There are people who you have to be careful with when you're giving negative feedback or constructive criticism. Harmesy is one of those. But he is also an incredibly selfless, team-first player.

For example, he was a first-choice mainstay in our midfield through 2016, 2017 and 2018, and was top five in the best and fairest in 2018. He was clearly seen as that 'next best' midfielder – after the superstars like Petracca and Oliver and Viney. But that's changed a little, and it's meant he's had to park his ego and play this role we call 'the mixed grill'. He basically plays almost every position on the ground, and has limited game time, too, because of how good the three guys in front of him are. It means Harmesy plays a little half-forward, a little wing, and a little longer on the bench than he would like, but all of it helps us win a premiership.

Monday to Friday is when he sometimes wavers about playing that role, because that's the time to have chats about your role, to ask questions, make your case and push for a little more. But when Friday night or Saturday afternoon rolls around, he is more focused and dialled in on the process than anyone. He tunes himself up and tunes right in.

There is no-one else like him on gameday. He gets into the rooms and bounces off the walls. He usually picks the music that's pumping. He's a rap and hip-hop man, and he sings it all, badly. In my captains speech, if I need someone to give us a joke or spark us up, Harmesy is my guy. Sometimes he messes it up, which is almost as funny, and it creates more of a laugh than the actual joke.

He's a lovely man. He's a Melbourne supporter, too, so he cares even more deeply for Demons fans. There's one in particular, a boy with Down syndrome, named John. I'm not sure how it happened but Harmesy found out that he is John's absolute favourite player, and immediately Harmesy wanted to acknowledge that. For years now he's gone to extra lengths to make this kid feel special. He gives him signed jumpers, says hi to him on the fence in the crowd, or searches for him after a win to give him the signed Sherrin from the match. Harmesy has been to John's house, and throughout 2020 he sent him videos during the season. If you asked John, he would say Harmesy is his best mate.

He's a good soul, and their bond is special, but it's worth noting that these kinds of things happen all the time in football. Players all over the league make special connections. We hear a lot of bad boy stories about footy players, and I understand that, because bad boy stories sell, and that's the landscape we live in. The John and Harmesy story doesn't sell newspapers, but for me personally – and I think most players – we know we can go to bed at night with our head on the pillow, comfortable that we've done some good in the world.

We felt that love come flowing back after the win against the Dogs. We had gathered some doubters in the days after the Adelaide loss – a bit of criticism from the experts that we struggle under pressure, from our skills to our game plan – which is a bit laughable when you're 9 and 1. But after that match at Marvel, they could see how we were holding our nerve this year – regaining top spot with an emphatic win against top opposition.

We had the weekend off, and I remember my phone really blowing up with excited messages from Melbourne supporters. And that was the first real sign that *their* belief was coming through. It carried on for the rest of the year, too, and carried us through a few low points. That game was the moment when it felt like things shifted outside our four walls, when the members had the same belief as we did, when they were thinking, 'That was electric', 'That was pure' and 'We can do this'.

CHAPTER 13

Round 12

Friday June 4, 7:50pm

Giants Stadium

Melbourne (14.13.97) versus Brisbane (11.9.75)

W hen it came to pandemic interruptions in 2021, we were very lucky as a football club, at least compared to others. I didn't enjoy flying to Tasmania on gameday against North Melbourne, but there were far worse fates for others. Some teams were forced to repeat stretches of 2020, staying in hubs away from family for weeks on end. Our inconveniences were just that – inconvenient but little more. Round 12 against the Brisbane Lions was one such inconvenience, when we had our venue changed from Alice Springs to Giants Stadium. The Northern Territory government just wouldn't let Melburnians in, so we ended up in Sydney for two nights.

Strange games in strange places seemed to be the growing theme of the season. This same round, the Blues hosted a 'home' game against the West Coast Eagles at the SCG, while the annual 'Dreamtime at the G' between the Tigers and the Bombers was held at Optus Stadium in Perth. All we could do was laugh, and be grateful that we could do our jobs, and venture farther from home than 5 km or 10 km or 15 km, or whatever restriction happened to be in place for our loved ones in Victoria.

It wasn't going to be an easy match. We may have felt strong coming off our win over the Dogs, but the Lions were putting together their own rich vein of form. Brisbane was on a seven-match winning streak, and had assembled what was – statistically at least – the most potent attack in the competition. They moved the ball quickly, and scored heavily. The big Joe Daniher and Eric Hipwood combo loomed large in the air. Charlie Cameron and Zac Bailey were strong on the deck. And their midfield was stacked with goalkickers, too, with the likes of Lachie Neale and Dayne Zorko and Hugh McCluggage.

We were right to be concerned – they were switched on from the first bounce. Hipwood and Daniher and Lincoln McCarthy were flying at everything. Charlie Cameron was dangerous at ground level, and Zac Bailey was, too. He's growing into a player, and kicked four goals. They seemed to be hunting us, too, isolating our defenders and attacking

ROUND 1: WIN

Coach Simon Goodwin addresses the team at half-time in the season's first match at the MCG. At half-time we were on track leading 7.6 to Fremantle's 3.8. It was a good start.

ROUND 2: WIN

Angus 'Gus' Brayshaw kicks the ball in a scrappy game against St Kilda. A player of great fortitude, who has overcome some potentially career-ending injuries, Gus was a key player through 2021.

ROUND 3: WIN

With his 20th birthday two months away, Kysaiah 'Kozzy' Pickett kicked four goals against Greater Western Sydney to establish his bona fides for the season with his speed, agility and strength.

ROUND 4: WIN

A four goal win over Geelong, and Christian Petracca at his best with 36 disposals and two goals.

ROUND 5: WIN

We won against Hawthorn by 50 points, kicking eight goals in the final quarter. It was a sign of things to come when we picked up some silverware: the Beyond Blue Cup.

ROUND 6: WIN

A win against the 2020 premiers, the Richmond Tigers, scoring 12.10 to 6.12 was a real boost for the team. As was the 300th game of former captain, Nathan Jones. Two milestones for club President Kate Roffey to enjoy.

ROUND 7: WIN

A solid win against North Melbourne in Tasmania, but tragedy struck when Adam Tomlinson was assisted off the ground. But 2021 proved our fitness and was not a big year for injuries.

ROUND 8: WIN

A resurgent Sydney failed to overwhelm us in a low-scoring match. Tom 'TMac' McDonald kicked four goals and Ben Brown, who debuted in Round 7 against his former club North Melbourne, kicked three goals that signalled what his value would be to Melbourne in 2021

ROUND 9: WIN

Ed Langdon makes his mark with 24 touches and a goal against Carlton.

ROUND 10: LOSS

Losing by one point, our nine-round winning streak ended. It turned out to be the last game for valued player Neville Jetta, who debuted for Melbourne in 2009 and played 159 games for the Demons.

ROUND 11: WIN

COVID-19 meant no crowds for the Demons match against the Western Bulldogs at Marvel Stadium. James Harmes contributed to our win and successfully nullified Tom Liberatore.

ROUND 12: WIN

With a 20-point lead at half-time, it looked like the Brisbane Lions were set to win, but by three-quarter time we had fought back to a one point difference. By the end of the match, we won by 22 points. It was an important win against a top team.

ROUND 13: LOSS

The Big Freeze banner says it all. Neale Daniher's courage and the memory of Jim Stynes were our inspiration to fight on throughout the season.

ROUND 15: WIN

After the loss to Collingwood and a bye, we were keen to focus up and reset. We won by 11 points as a valiant Essendon battled for a win.

ROUND 16: LOSS

GWS came out hard but even though we lost, it was only by nine points. Trent Rivers (pictured), Luke Jackson and 'Kozzy' Pickett were part of a hugely successful draft haul for the club. Trent Rivers played every match for the season, as did Pickett, and Jackson only missed one.

ROUND 17: WIN

Our first outing against Port Adelaide was always going to be a test, especially in Adelaide, but we nailed it with a 31-point win. Harrison Petty defended well and proved he was made of the right stuff.

them, no more so than the always fiery Mitch Robinson laying out Jake Lever. By half-time they were 20 points in front, they had 14 more inside 50s, 11 more contested possessions and eight more clearances. They were belting us.

But we stopped that in the third quarter, and we stopped it with our own offence, which people often forget is the best way to defend. Keeping the ball in your forward half is just about the single best way to avoid having goals kicked against you. Those worrying half-time stats were turned completely on their head. In the second half we had 17 more inside 50s, 16 more contested possessions and 10 more clearances. We kicked nine out of 12 goals, and won by 22 points.

But how does that happen? How do you arrest momentum, and then push back the other way? We started by creating a really simple centre-bounce plan, and became more efficient going forward, so we scored goals a little easier. I remember Petracca putting on a show as well, which always helps. You can also put a lot down to maturity. The Demons of another era probably wouldn't win this contest, but changing the script within a game – refusing to be hunted, and instead doing the hunting – that's something the likes of defensive coach Troy Chaplin have been drilling into us for a few years now. There must be a real pleasure for him in watching those things come to fruition.

This became another one of those games we returned to throughout the rest of the season. We added it to that list, and I'm glad we did. We literally talked about this game in the Grand Final, at half-time. In both matches we were down by three goals, completely outplayed in some parts of the game, but dominating in other parts. We knew what we had to do against the Dogs because we had done it against the Lions. Goody talked about the importance of that Lions game immediately to media. He could see how crucial it was, not only to consolidate our win from the week before, but to have responded when challenged. He called it 'one of the most consequential games of the year', and he was spot on.

Some people wondered whether fitness was a factor in that win, and others, and it's a good question, given how well we ran out games all season long – emphatically so in the finals. I look back and remember how I always had such negative feelings about running, for most of my career. I used to go into games not worried about playing against a guy like Nic Naitanui – who is just so strong and so good at football – but I would go into a game against Matthew Kreuzer petrified, because he could run all day. It was a strange thing, but I felt that most weeks. I wasn't concerned about taking on a legend like Dean Cox, but I was scared stiff of keeping up with Todd Goldstein. And the weird thing was that I'd actually perform well against

Kreuzer and Goldstein, and get smashed by Nic Nat and utterly outplayed by Cox. It was a strange mindset, which has now come full 360.

I used to dread any running program – I just didn't like running. But now I enjoy it. For the past three off-seasons, I've actually come to love running. I'm lucky that I've changed it into a strength. I think I can now defend those rucks who can run, and can even take some guys apart with my running. I don't worry about it anymore at all, and I reckon that frees me up to think about other parts of the game. I don't know what's changed exactly. It might just be my mental view on fitness.

Six years ago things were really different for me in that space. When Mark Neeld came in as coach, he wanted to do things a certain way. He wanted us all incredibly fit, and that's no different than any coach. But he wanted everyone to be under a specific mark for a time trial. Basically, if you wanted to play in the midfield, you had to do the three-kilometre time trial in under 10 minutes and 20 seconds. And we had some really good midfielders who were outside of 10:20 – guys like Brent Moloney, James Magner, Colin Sylvia and Tom Couch. These were big, strong boys, but they weren't the strongest runners. We had another guy, Jordan Gysberts, who was a really high draft pick with heaps of talent, but he was clearly outside 10:20. And because of that, there was a year where he didn't get to play until about Round 15, when he finally nudged under that 10:20 mark. It was meant to be this aspirational target, but in some ways it made us fixate on the idea that bad runners were bad players.

I remember a moment from that year when it all became clear to me. Dan Nicholson, a good friend of mine, ran a 9:10 for the three-kilometre time trial, which is just so far off the scale. And he played midfield for us, coming into a game against Geelong to tag Steve Johnson. Now, I don't know if Stevie J can run, but he doesn't scream at me as someone who can run a 9:10. But nevertheless, Stevie J kicked five goals and had 30-odd touches. And I began to think that maybe you don't need to be able to run 9:10 to play this game.

We were all so fit. Incredibly fit. I have personal bests from that era that I will never, ever hit again. Not a chance. My body composition, skin folds and running times were so far ahead of what they are now. All our numbers were incredible, but we were clearly missing something that would help us use that stamina. Maybe belief?

Over the past decade, fitness bosses have become all the rage in the AFL. But in my mind, they're all the same in some ways – they've all done the same courses, and the majority have similar experiences, and they harbour goals for players that aren't that different. Where they become important probably comes back to belief. It's about how they convey messages and get players to trust them. I think that's what was so important for us about Darren Burgess, our high-performance boss for the past two years. Belief.

We might not have been fitter than the teams we were playing against this year, but we *thought* we were. That's Burgo's talent – getting everyone to trust his program and not waver. His quote is 'Round 1 will come, and you'll think you've worked harder than the bloke you're up against', and at the time you go, 'I won't think that.' But then we got to Round 1 and I thought, 'Yep, we're definitely fitter than these guys.'

Does being fitter matter? In some ways fitness is a very small thing – far less important than your ability with the football in hand. Usually the more skilful side wins. But maybe fitness feeds into this mental state you need to reach in order to win. Put it this way, there were times this year when we were challenged, but we just *knew* we were going to outrun sides. We felt it in our bodies. Maybe it's not belief – maybe it's faith. We had faith in Burgo.

It helps that he came to us with a reputation. He's thought of everywhere as the 'best in the business' and gets called a 'fitness guru' and an 'off-field architect', and that breeds a certain confidence in what he does. He's worked with the Socceroos, with Port Adelaide, with Premier League heavyweights Liverpool and Arsenal, and was on the AFL reality TV show *The Recruit*. But funnily enough, he's never actually won anything until now. Whatever he's done to improve the fitness of lists hasn't led to the ultimate success – until now. What didn't quite work for them clearly worked for us. I guess he was the right man at the right time to convey the right message.

He also brought new talent with him. Because of his lofty place in the industry, people want to work with him. If you're a fitness staffer, it's good to have experience with Darren Burgess on your résumé. So we got some of the best of the best to come to us from different clubs – and countries – because they wanted to work alongside Burgo and learn from his methods. Selwyn Griffith left the Brisbane Lions after eight years to come and work with Burgo. Our new head of sport science, David Regan, left his job with the Miami Dolphins in the NFL to work with Burgo. David Watts, our weights coach, left Geelong for the same reason. Burgo has actually just left Melbourne after two years, after the flag, to go home to Adelaide for family reasons – border restrictions having kept him apart from his kids for almost two years. But his time with us has set systems in place, and left us with his highly credentialled core group of industry leaders to take things forward. So much trust has been built.

A small example is the way niggles were treated. Football departments can be obsessive about players' bodies, but over the past two years we haven't had those long medical meetings, and no endless discussion of injuries – he brought in this new way where a problem is assessed and dealt with quick smart: 'This is the issue, this is what we're doing, and this is how we'll do it.' I didn't have any injuries this year but I had a few sessions where I was a bit sore, and his team just got inside your head and got you into such a great mental state. Players want fitness staff to say 'You'll be right', and they said 'You'll be right', which is a dangerous thing for a physio or doctor to say, because if they're wrong, it comes back onto them.

The treatment of Steven May after he pulled his hamstring in the preliminary final is the perfect example. He tweaked it, and he knew it, but nobody fed into any alarm about it. He trained, and ran, and it wasn't 100 per cent, but there was this faith placed in the player and the staff to figure out what to do. All anyone wanted to know was 'Did Steve have faith in his leg?' and 'Did our fitness staff have faith in his leg?' and 'Did our medical staff have faith in his leg?' That system is now set, meaning Burgo can leave, and the other guys can remain and add their own touches, knowing the way we do things. Belief. Faith. Trust.

Of course, it's not just high-profile guys like Burgo who matter in this space. As professional footballers, we spend an awful lot of time in the gym, in changing rooms, in medical suites – laying down on benches and strapping tables. You speak to a lot of guys who've retired from footy and that's what they say they miss most – sitting around inside before or after a session, shooting the breeze with the guys and girls who keep us in peak physical shape. We spend huge amounts of time with the people who rub out those niggling sore spots, or tape up our injuries, or measure our skin folds. People like John Stanaway.

John came to the club in the 1990s, when football clubs were light on the ground for medical professionals. Each club probably had a part-time doctor, maybe a full-time physio, and a head trainer – and that's a guy who's got his first aid certificate, and perhaps he knows a little myotherapy, and he knows how to tape ankles. That was John – head trainer and jack of all trades – and he's been that person for us for more than 20 years. He was there for the 2000 Grand Final. He had his 450th game this year.

He used to be one of the guys who ran onto the ground during games, running water and checking us after collisions, helping us off the field if needed, but now he's got crook ankles and sits on the bench. Now his role is to come to main training, tape ankles and talk shit. And come to the game, tape ankles and talk shit. If someone gets concussed or has a bad injury, John's the guy who sits with them in the rooms, who takes care of them. He's a helper-outerer. Football clubs are built on people like that.

And it's important to remember them, because it got harder and harder to have volunteers at football clubs during the pandemic, as we couldn't have people coming into the club who were working elsewhere, because it increased that risk of exposure. But we stayed strong with John, because of the person he is and also because of his connection to past players and past moments – to the history of the club.

When we flew to Western Australia for the preliminary final and the flag, we could only bring a crew of 75. We had to leave many people behind – from staff members to board members to volunteers. But John got the nod to come along. To see the smile on his face when he finally saw a premiership made it all worth it. It was important to involve people like him in that trip, to take them out on the road with us in that moment, because more than anyone else they know the journey we've been on.

CHAPTER 14

Round 13

Monday June 14, 3:20pm

Sydney Cricket Ground

Melbourne (9.9.63) versus Collingwood (11.14.80)

This was the worst game of the year. If you look at our projected scores – a Champion Data prediction of who will win based on all the statistics, including all of the players on the field that day, with every little numeric thing you can imagine taken into account – we're literally meant to win this contest against Collingwood 24 times out of 25. But this was that one other time – the 25th version of the game. Against the 16th-placed Magpies, the predicted likelihood of us winning was 96 per cent, but we completely bottled it. In fact we beat every team this year *except* Collingwood.

I look back now on how we handled it, and there were mistakes. We were in Sydney a week earlier to play Brisbane, but came home and then flew up again – maybe we should have just stayed? Did we underestimate the Magpies – who were playing for their coach, Nathan Buckley, in his last game? Could we have placed too much importance on the round, and not enough on the match itself? Sometimes you can't tell exactly where a loss comes from. All I know is something stunk a little before the game, stunk a little during the day, and definitely stunk a lot after the game.

The Magpies showed their run and daring, and they refused to bomb the ball into their forward line, making Lever and May as accountable as possible and taking away our intercept weapons. They led by 16 at half-time, and although we closed to within five points in the last quarter, they won by 17 in the end. Collingwood played wonderfully, we played horribly, and when you put those two together, the outcome is a three-goal defeat. Apparently even in the middle of a dream season, the new Melbourne could still be the old Melbourne.

It's hard to describe how disappointed I was. When I got to the club, the Queen's Birthday game was talked up as our Grand Final, in place of actual grand finals. It's one of those games that's big no matter what, filled with upsets, and where ladder position counts for less than ever, and where everything that happens is magnified.

Just ask Jack Watts. It was the Queen's Birthday game in 2009 when he debuted, too soon it turned out, and was monstered verbally and physically by senior Magpies. Jack talks now about how he was 'thrown to the wolves' that afternoon. He was a big part of the story much later, too, in 2017, when he was one of the best players on the field in a close game, which we won. We missed out on playing finals that year by 0.5 per cent.

There are many more stories around that Monday public holiday game, but they tend to have faded in importance alongside what the day has become, and alongside the man who built that day up. I'm talking of course about former coach Neale Daniher, and the Big Freeze at the G.

While we were in Sydney, Neale was at the MCG, holding his annual fundraiser for motor neurone disease, the disease that's got its claws into him. It's become one of the most important events on the football calendar – a pandemic wasn't about to stop it going ahead. There were no crowds, and no game, and it was overcast and windy, but the slide and the icy pool below it were ready for an assortment of celebrities. Billy Brownless, Daisy Pearce, Abbey Holmes, Sarah Jones, Sharni Norder and Craig Bellamy all took the plunge in costume.

Shane Crawford dressed as Queen Elizabeth. 'Razor' Ray Chamberlain was Elton John. Gillon McLachlan was Meat Loaf. Russel Howcroft, a Dees fan, went down topless with a red and blue heart painted on his chest. Jeff 'The Wizard' Farmer was in tears afterwards. The campaign – led by Neale, who now struggles to speak, and who one day earlier was appointed an Officer of the Order of Australia – has now raised more than $60 million to fund research into the disease and make life better for those with it.

Neale is – without a doubt – the most selfless person I know. We've talked about the selflessness of the ANZACs. Neale is the definition of that spirit. Think about it for a second. He's fighting a battle that he is *not* going to win, so that *others* can try to win it. He talks about that, too, every time he comes into the club. Those are his messages – selfless versus selfish, walking the walk or talking the talk. He's big on sharing mottos – his own is 'Play On' – and we always come away so inspired.

I had a great moment with him in the off-season a few years ago, after a golf day down on the Mornington Peninsula with a bunch of the younger players. We went to the Sorrento house of a board member and former president, Don McLardy. Neale was there. Jack Watts and I came back from hitting the links, and we found Don with Neale. It was just the two of them around the campfire, listening to tunes. We sat down, and they said they were playing a game. You had to put a song on the playlist without telling anyone what it was, and then as the tracks shuffle and play, you have to guess whose song is whose.

The first song that came on was 'Happy' by Bruno Mars. We were all pretty sure that was Wattsy. But it was Neale. And he went into why he liked it. He said he didn't know what the words were about, or what it meant, or who the singer was – it just made him smile. He sat there jiggling around, clapping along. That was a great moment to have with a guy who could hardly say anything.

Since then we've become friends, Neale and I. We text. He's come into the club a few times this year, too. His son is now speaking for him. His daughter spoke for him at the Big Freeze this year. But he still communicates himself – he has that big grin, and a kind of cheeky look in his eye. My one regret is I didn't get a chance to know him before he was sick. I can only imagine what he was like when he was healthy and well.

He's important to the club, though, for more than inspiration. He's a connector. I talk a lot about involving past players from Melbourne, and there is literally no stronger connection within a former side than the playing group that Neale Daniher coached. They didn't win a flag in 2000 – they lost – but they are just so bonded.

Many of my teammates who have gone to other clubs, come back to the Melbourne past players group over any other. On days like the Queen's Birthday Monday, you know they're all watching, too. You know the pressure is on, and you want to do justice to them. They deserve it.

Melbourne is in many ways a club bound together by modern tragedy. The list of people who have passed away too young is so long.

Robbie Flower.

Steven Armstrong.

Colin Sylvia.

Sean Wight.

Troy Broadbridge.

Dean Bailey.

And of course there's one more.

I knew Jim Stynes only when he was sick. He was diagnosed with metastatic melanoma – brain cancer – in 2009, the year I was drafted. I remember he was quoted in a newspaper saying he was excited about this young tall kid they were bringing into the club, and the next day we did a tour of the MCG, six young draftees with our families, and he sits us all in a room, and he goes, 'Who's that big fella in the back?' I stood up. 'This guy is the one I'm most excited about,' he said, bearing in mind I was in a room with Tom Scully and Jack Trengove, picks 1 and 2. 'This guy is the guy.' And right then I knew we had a special connection.

Jim wanted me to do things differently, my own way, and I think I have. He did things extremely differently himself, so any time I'm making a decision and taking something in a new direction, I think back on him. I think how he came from Ireland, played 240 games in a row, with broken backs and hurt legs, how he started a charity for underprivileged youths who were mentally challenged in their teens. That's so far out of the norm, particularly back then. Anything I do that seems odd is not even half as strange as what Jim did. I was also a pretty raw teen growing up, but Stynesy just let me be me, and he shared a pretty important message: that it's OK to be the person you want to be.

I look at his jumper – his number 11 – every time before I play. I get it out of my locker, and as I'm about to put it on, I look at the logo and think about how Melbourne is the oldest club in Australia, one of the oldest in the world, and I realise who I'm playing for, and it's not for myself, it's for all these supporters. Then I flip it over to look at the back and see the number 11, and that gives me my own individual focus. His little motto was 'Whatever it takes', and I know that's a common one – it was even used by Essendon before their supplements saga – but when I look at my jumper, I hear it out of Jim's mouth. I hear it in his voice. Jim drank his own urine to try to stay alive – he explained that all the vitamins boosted his immune system. He was the ultimate 'Whatever it takes' man. I'm just playing a game of footy, but I hear him saying 'Whatever it takes', and I bring that out onto the field.

Of course, that's not the only moment that connects me and him and the Melbourne guernsey. Jim presented me with my first jumper, when it was my turn to debut. It was number 37 – that was his first number at the club, too – and he gave it to me on a Wednesday. That's not the norm, of course. Usually you get your jumper on the weekend, in the minutes leading up to the match. But Jim couldn't be there that weekend, because he was going in for brain surgery.

As a young kid, I'm not sure I understood that moment. Jim was a four-time best-and-fairest, a Brownlow Medallist, a true champion with his own charity, and to me he was the president of the footy club. But I look back now, and I realise that this was just a guy, a man, a sick man, getting up off his deathbed to come down to Casey Fields and present me with my jumper, because that's how much he loved footy, and the club, and because he thought and hoped that I was going to be a good player.

He gave this speech, about being your own man, and walking your own path. It was taped at the time. I watch it every now and then. 'I want to wish you all the best,' he said, 'because football is going to do some good things for you. But one thing I wanted to say is, "Don't ever take it for granted. Because it can disappear faster – much faster – than it's come."'

Jim died nine months later.

Have I taken anything for granted? Has it disappeared faster than I imagined? Everyone says that when you retire, your career flashes before your eyes. That's the big final speech – I've heard a few – about how it all goes so quickly. But I've enjoyed every minute and I've made sure I've experienced every minute. Even when we've struggled, I've loved being a footballer.

I've lived as true a life as I could. And when I finish up I think it'll feel like a big part of my life – a massive part of my life – and it hasn't gone that quickly at all. I've listened to those words from Jim, and I think of him and I think of Neale, too, and I know what I would tell an 18-year-old coming into the system. I'd say 'Be you, live like you, and you'll enjoy this experience exactly as you should.'

CHAPTER 15

Round 14

Mid-season bye

Normally in a bye round, football players scatter. It's one of the few times during the year you'll have an extended moment away from the club, and everyone uses it differently. Ed Langdon likes to go where no-one can find him. Immediately after the Grand Final, for instance, he went to Fitzroy Crossing, four hours inland from Broome, to go hunting and fishing, but during the bye he just got in a car and headed north. I have no idea where he went. I'm not sure anyone does. Christian Petracca is a different beast. He loves a night out, which I think he got in Sydney. Simon Goodwin stayed in New South Wales, too, for a little holiday away from everything. We've got campers among us, like Jake Lever and Alex Neal-Bullen, who just need to go bush and breathe. Oskar Baker goes to Brisbane every chance he gets. He's from Brisbane, loves Brisbane, thinks he's the king of Brisbane.

But we're a really big family club – there are nine dads among us, which is well above the norm. I think the Bulldogs team we played against in the Grand Final had one dad. Being about to become a dad, I came back to Melbourne, and stayed at home. I like to use that moment to press pause and relax a little in the middle of any season.

It's funny, though, because while it's good to refresh, I also find it extremely hard to get back to the right level of fitness. Four days off sounds like nothing, but it can slow the machine down a bit, and it's hard to get it revving again. Skip an entire week of training and you feel sluggish immediately. That's what happens when such a large part of your life is about daily physical performance. Don't get me started on how difficult it is when you're returning from injury. For that reason I kept moving, persuading Steven May to come down and see me and have a run around Rye Oval.

Once we gathered again as a group, though, we didn't go straight back into our weekly routine. There was one more thing we needed to do. We needed to revisit that meeting we had at the golf course in Cranbourne in the pre-season – the 'players only' gathering where we hashed out what we wanted this season to look like, and what we needed to demand from one another to make it happen. We always knew we would come back to it mid-year – it just so happened to be after our worst game of the year. It was quite handy in a way, to have that second session when we did, because we were able to talk about the big picture stuff that gets lost in the day-to-day life of footy season.

We weren't allowed to play golf because of COVID, so we met at the Lido cinemas on Glenferrie Road in Hawthorn, and we watched *Fast and Furious 9*. There was no real reason behind the choice. I haven't watched the first eight, and I won't watch the next eight if they keep making them. The only person who liked it was Tom McDonald, because he loves cars and has seen all eight of them. He almost gave it a standing ovation. We were thinking of paying to get a cameo video from Vin Diesel – Tommy would have loved that.

The movie wasn't the point though – the point was the gathering afterwards. We huddled up in small groups in the foyer there, and talked about following up what we had set in stone all those months ago. And that's when a lot of people started saying, 'We're a chance – we've put ourselves in a good position, so why not us?'

You don't just walk around the change rooms saying, 'We'll win it this year.' You need a safe space for those conversations. This was that – a chance to talk about how you were feeling. I mentioned to the boys that we were in a position to do something special this year. It wasn't a long meeting – we didn't need that. It was just a consolidation. And it helped us realise the Collingwood game was a blip – an aberration – and not a reversion to type.

It would be wrong to say that the gathering at the movies was pivotal, and sent us soaring through the latter part of the season, because we definitely had some poor games later in the year. A bit came up about losing to teams below us – which was Adelaide and Collingwood – and how that reminded us of those losses in Cairns last year to Sydney and Fremantle. It reminded us about respecting the game and respecting the opposition.

It was one of those little things you look back on, and add up alongside so many other moments, and you begin to realise that there's this cumulative effect of all of those moments combined. We wouldn't have done what we did if we hadn't talked like we did in the hub last season, if we hadn't thrashed everything out like we did in pre-season, and if we hadn't re-examined all of that like we did mid-season – in the bye. I think that meeting is where a few slow-twitch fibres got sparked, and maybe that helped us catch fire later. Sometimes the little things are everything.

CHAPTER 16

Round 15

Saturday June 26, 7:25pm

Melbourne Cricket Ground

Essendon (8.9.57) versus Melbourne (9.14.68)

After the bye, I know our fans were afraid of a mini-slump, or maybe something worse. Countless teams have stormed through the first half of the season only for the wheels to fall off on the run home. We had just lost two games out of four, and were facing a tough test against a rising side. I wish I could say we were supremely confident inside the club, but we weren't.

We had a massive training session during the bye, and we all felt a little cooked afterwards, and that sort of carried into that Essendon game. Physically, it was just a dour contest. Essendon were really good defensively. I definitely remember walking off that ground at half-time thinking that the bloody bye round had got to me again.

I'd come out feeling more fatigued than ever, and I was up against a young ruck that I really rate, Sam Draper. He's come a long way – like I did – with knee reconstructions, and I had been excited to have a little battle with him and their midfield. Darcy Parish and Zach Merrett were flying. Jake Stringer was causing us issues – leaving the centre bounce and going forward straight away. We knew he would do that, but still, there's this 20 seconds where a midfielder has to be accountable for Stringer until Michael Hibberd can get to him in defence, and we were missing that link.

It was just a low-scoring, scrappy, shit game. We played some pretty good football in the third quarter, and that was the match. We won by 11 points. Petracca was our best with 26 disposals and two goals. Oliver had 34 and six clearances. James Jordon was great with 21 touches and two goals. One of them was a huge moment for us – it came off a 100-metre penalty, when we had really been struggling to score. It was one of those matches that's so important to tick off. You know you're off, you know the other team is coming, but you also know you need to win. It wasn't pretty, but it was gutsy, determined, professional football, and it reminds me of one player: Nathan Jones.

This was game number 302 for Jonesy, and although he won't see it as a last game, that's what the record books will show. He sat on the bench that day, as the unused medical sub. It's such a strange quirk that a rule change brought in this season means a champion of our footy club plays his last game without touching the ball, without leaving the sideline. He got injured at training a week later, before our match against Greater Western Sydney. It was a calf injury. A one-week absence turned into two, and he couldn't quite get back into the team or make his case until closer to finals, when a team on top seldom makes any changes to its side. It's unfair, for such a player and such a person to have it end this way, but that's football.

I remember when I first walked into the club, Jonesy was actually a bit of a larrikin. He had the scope to be a really good leader, but he was in the leadership group at the time mostly because he was genuinely talented. He grew into the role quickly though. He hit me up as soon as I got there. On my first Christmas break I came in to do weights. I thought I was doing the right thing, extras, working hard, coming into the Junction Oval on time off. He walked in and asked the weights coach – *just loud enough so he knew I could hear* – if I was doing everything I should. I was in the middle of a bench press and I'm laying there thinking, 'Jesus, this guy's a prick, I've come in on my break to do some lifting and he's making a mockery of me.' But he knew that I was a bit of a coaster early on, and he could read that, and this was his way of making sure I didn't coast – that I understood extras were the norm, and not something that gets a pat on the back. He wasn't someone to sit there and watch me cruise; he was going to make sure I cracked in and did my bit for the team.

And from there on we actually became really good friends. I got invited to his wedding in only my third year. You might have this impression from the outside that you're best mates with all 45 guys on the list, because you spend all that time together, bonded by a common purpose. And you are, but it's also like any school or workplace. Some people are closer than others. Weddings are the events where you can really see what's going on, because you just can't invite every single player and their partner. I think I was only a late-round invite after a declined RSVP, but I got there, and that was around the time he had become captain, and I felt like I was right there with him, trying to turn the ship around, trying to learn everything I could from the way he conducts himself.

It starts with training and physical preparation. Apart from this season, I can't really remember Jonesy getting injured. He just trains and trains and trains. His best and fairest numbers are phenomenal – he seems to finish in the top five every year – and that comes back to consistency, and application, and routine. He's just attentive to everything in his preparation. But the thing I find even more staggering is the way he time-trials. Again, I think he's been in the top five his whole career. This year he was third behind Adam Tomlinson and Fraser Rosman, who are both 6 foot 4 endurance animals. You can only pull that off at 33 years old if you're consistently elite in the way you take care of your body.

Even at the end of this season, when he had played seven games and was probably in his own mind about to retire, I remember going into his room in the Perth hub ahead of the preliminary final, and we were sitting there watching television, and he's got all this protein powder and beetroot juice, and he had his foam roller out, and his pilates mat, and his compression pants – those things you turn on and they bulge and compress your legs for better recovery. I haven't seen him eat a bad meal. Ever. He's just someone who's incredibly consistent with that stuff, and you would think that not getting picked at the end of your career, you might ease up – but not him. He gets everything out of himself, always.

There are some good photos of him from when he was drafted, and he's still got hair and just a few tattoos, then the sleeve happened early, and now of course he's got all that ink. His appearance probably doesn't scream 'family man' either, but you have to see him up close with his kids. His first two go to a college, and I love the thought of him doing the school pickup with his new twins, walking there with a pram, wearing his muscle tee and shorts, bald head, full tatts. I can imagine people might be a bit standoffish in that situation, but I'm sure once he smiles and opens his mouth all that changes. He's the most devoted dad, and those kids worship him, following him everywhere he goes. They'll both probably play footy in the end, regardless of how much natural talent they've got, simply because they just want to do what Dad does.

It's hard to say how he felt through the down years at the club. I think he and I have always thought we would wait until we were done with football to have that conversation. I'm certain he would have been looking at silver linings all throughout, but everyone's got an ego in football, and the team's lack of success would have really hurt him. He would have seen guys from his draft year like Grant Birchall and Scott Pendlebury and Josh Kennedy playing in regular finals and winning premierships. But it just shows the person he is, how he is able to hold himself to such a high level, even as the team was performing so poorly. There's only so much one player can do to try and resurrect a team, and I think he did everything he could.

He wasn't just a leader by example, either. He's a great speaker, too. It's strange, because he's a bit of a bogan, but his ability to convey a message is the best I've seen. He should almost be a politician. Whenever I've had trouble speaking as captain, I always just go, 'Nathan, can you help me out here and say what needs to be said?' We could talk in a meeting for three hours, going over and over stuff, and no-one getting the right thing out, and then Nathan finally opens his mouth and says one sentence, and we all go, 'Yep, that's it, got it.' If you watch him do any media work you realise how thorough he is, and how his understanding of the game is complete.

'Chunk' likes to point out how early on in his captaincy, there was a black-or-white school of leadership – my way or the highway – and it was all about strength. And he had to grow up a little, or grow into the new age, to understand how to embrace differences and look at things from other perspectives. I think I probably had that last part in my toolkit already – but I didn't have the first part, and you need some of that, too. I learned from Nathan how to lead from the front, how to get guys to line up behind you and follow your actions. You can be a new age thinker, but you still need to be an old school leader. I had my own strength in being able to make people feel comfortable around me, but I didn't necessarily have that strength to make people come with me. He taught me that.

There are a few ways to look at the end of Nathan's career. You could say he was thinking about retiring but went on another year, got seven games and reached his 300, and saw his team win a flag. That's a pretty good way to end.

Another way to look at it is saying he was very unlucky to be out of the team, because of injury, and then very unlucky that he couldn't get his way back in, whether through injuries or the VFL schedule, and then very unlucky in the timing of the birth of his twins, and the state of pandemic border restrictions meaning if he left Perth for their birth, he couldn't come back even if he was selected, meaning he knew he was about to be locked out of the state to watch his team play in a grand final and possibly win a flag. That's a pretty sad way to end.

But here's the thing, whichever way you look at it his story is an extraordinary one, and I think that's something we can all take away from the career of Nathan Jones. His legend isn't going to recede. He's a 16-year veteran of the Melbourne Football Club, one who led through the toughest times and who set the standards we now live by – the standards that won us a premiership. He didn't get the send-off or the farewell he deserved, but he would know that deep down every single Melbourne supporter is grateful for what he did, and that gratitude is shared by all the players. I'm the captain of the club right now, and someone will take over from me one day, and someone else will take over from them, but I guarantee you they'll call Jonesy their skipper, because that's what he is to all of us. To me and the team, he's skip for life.

CHAPTER 17

Round 16

Saturday July 3, 1:45pm

Melbourne Cricket Ground

Melbourne (7.13.55) versus Greater Western Sydney (9.10.64)

There's no sugarcoating a loss like this. On days like this you can blame inaccuracy – we kicked 7.13. Or you can talk about efficiency going forward – in the last quarter we managed only 2.4 from 18 entries. But in the end, this was our first defeat at the MCG since 2019, we were smashed at clearances the entire first half, the Giants kept us in it by missing their own chances in the third quarter, and we hit the lead once all day, for three short minutes in the first quarter. Toby Greene, Josh Kelly and Jacob Hopper led the way for them, while Petracca, Salem and Fritsch kept us in touch. But we didn't deserve to win.

That's not to say this was a shock. Good opposition is good opposition, and GWS were flying at this stage. In truth this match always presented to us as a danger game, and we might have been thinking too much about the week prior. We left the game against Essendon going, 'Damn, that was tough.' We had won by 11 points but the Bombers could have easily won it, too, and that's how we walked off the ground, and we probably didn't correct ourselves going into the challenge against the Giants. We stayed in that state, in that mindset.

And GWS were hot – they were all over us. We went back to a few old habits where we try and get too many people over the ball, and everyone wants to get the Sherrin. The numbers show that we worked incredibly hard, but the Giants worked smarter. The last quarter went completely our way – we had six shots, but bellied every snap, and could have won it late – but they were able to hold on. They outdid us, outplayed us.

You can't win games in last quarters – or at least you shouldn't put yourself in a position to rely on winning games in last quarters – especially when a team is in full defensive mode like they were. That Giants game taught us that we weren't quite there with fully understanding all our roles when a team throws something different our way. You need to make the game play out the way you intend even when the opposition surprises you; you need to know how to adjust the dials.

That becomes really important when playing teams

that are below you on the ladder, who think they need to close a kind of performance gap to beat you. Put it this way: when you have two top-four teams playing against one another, those teams tend just to back their system to win. It becomes a battle of strength versus strength. But when you play sides that are developing or catching up or getting on a run from the lower part of the ladder, they often try to take something specific away from you. They do a fair bit more oppo analysis, and try to get inside your game, whether it's taking away your key marking players, or smothering your midfield ball use.

There was one player, however, who stood out to me that day for his composure. Trent Rivers had 22 possessions, 15 of them kicks, and it's in that sort of performance that you began to see what he's evolving into as a player. I describe him as a footballer, not an athlete, and I hope that doesn't come across as a slight on his physical attributes, because it's not. He's simply got a footballer's brain on him. He actually has an amazing physique for a half-back, in that I think he can play on both talls and smalls going forward. That's a handy person to have on your list, in the same mould as a Nick Vlastuin or Tom Stewart. I feel like he's going to be that player for us one day, but at the moment – because he's got so much youth and athleticism – he's that dashing half-back for us, and in this game I remember he almost won it for us late with a couple of key disposals.

He was taken by us with pick 32 in the 2019 draft, of course, with Luke Jackson at 3 and Kozzy Pickett at 12 – three Western Australian boys taken together. He was nominated for the Rising Star Award for his game against the Western Bulldogs, too, and just stamped himself as a best-22 player for us all year. Now, Jacko won the entire Rising Star Award, and Kozzy is Kozzy, but I'm almost the most excited by Trent, because he's the one who's gone slightly under the radar, yet played all 25 games in a crucial part of the ground. The hardest trust you can win at our club is that of Steven May, and I think he's got it already.

Trent plays with a bit of swagger, too, which I love. You can tell that he feels like he belongs. Jake Bowey is a bit the same. They both like to express themselves on the football field, and it's interesting to see that in young defenders. The young guys want to show their flair, and are as excited about kicking the footy as defending through spoils. It's a sign of the times.

It's also great to see the recruiting team lauded for selections like Trent, and Jake, not to mention Jacko and Kozzy, because it's been such a long road for us as a club through the draft over the years. We've had so many high draft picks, and so often they've been cruelled or stunted by injury or mishap, to the point that there's this long list of names that our fans can't help but think of and wonder what might have been, whether Scully or Trengove,

Toumpas or Tapscott, Gysberts or Morton, Watts or Blease, Petterd or Cook. Throughout our entire rebuild our list management team has been called into question, whether trading out pick 2 in 2013 (which became Josh Kelly) for Dom Tyson and Christian Salem, or even the first-round draft picks spent to bring May and Jake Lever to the team. As recently as two years ago, immediately after the 2019 draft, people were all too willing to believe we had messed it up by bringing in Jackson, Pickett and Rivers. We've been vindicated now, of course, but still, people tend to pick apart draft choices in hindsight, looking only through the old retrospectoscope.

I'm still not sure people really understand the way drafting and development are intertwined, and how the state of the club when a young draftee arrives plays a part in what they become. Take a guy like Jack Watts. Every single club takes Jack Watts as either pick 1 or pick 2, 100 per cent of the time. Every single club takes Jimmy Toumpas in their top 10. Most of the guys who Melbourne fans will remember as hot prospects that didn't quite make it would be able to play in the teams that we fielded this year. If they were still in the squad while we made this journey together, I'm sure a lot of those players would have been able to adapt and play in a premiership team as well.

They came to the club at a bad time. Yes, there are a few success stories from that era, like Nathan Jones and Neville

Jetta. There's myself and Tom McDonald, too, but we were almost lucky because we were seen as project players. They might have given us the flick early on, but perhaps we stayed because we had a bit of height. We're both quite lucky that we survived that era. Now, thanks to guys in our list team like Jason Taylor and Tim Lamb, we're bringing in the right people, who get to work within the right culture, and keep the club moving in the right direction.

But for the players who came before them, you just can't tell what would have happened if circumstances had been a little different. Stefan Martin went to another club and played against us in a grand final. Ricky Petterd left and played some good footy elsewhere. Sam Blease and Jordie Gysberts went to other clubs but I think old Melbourne just got to them – they were worn down by their experience. Trengove kept playing, and so did Watts, and both looked like they could be something but were beaten in the end by broken bones.

There will always be these kinds of stories in football, of skilled and hopeful kids who could have been serious players but were drafted to the wrong place at the wrong time. Footy can be fickle in that way. We like to pretend that everything comes down to effort and desire and talent, but there are pretty random forces in play as well. There's a lot of luck in footy. You just have to hope you get more good than bad.

CHAPTER 18

Round 17

Thursday July 8, 7:10pm

Adelaide Oval

Port Adelaide (8.7.55) versus Melbourne (12.14.86)

My magnet must have been circled on the Port Adelaide whiteboard. You can tell when that's happened, based on the physical attention you get from the opposition. It actually tends to happen every time I play against their ruckman, Scott Lycett, but he did come pretty hard at me on this Thursday night. It doesn't bother me though, to be honest. It's part of the game. Every club does it, including us.

Basically it involves constant bumping. Other times an opponent stands in front of you, blocking your run, just forcing you to run a few extra metres with every play, hoping to wear you out over the course of the game. Sometimes they hold you down when you're at the base of a pack, forcing you to spend that little bit more energy getting up off the deck. I'm not sure if it's effective.

When I'm watching another game and see it, I don't blink an eyelid. It's like, 'Oh, they're targeting so-and-so tonight. That's interesting.' When it's happening to you, of course, you do get a bit worked up at times, and maybe try to throw your own weight around in response, but really, if your side is going as well as what we were in that game against the Power, then I don't really care.

But it does happen more with some teams and players than others. I remember Lycett went to me in the 2018 preliminary final, when he was playing for West Coast, and we got smashed in that game. In the very next game, Round 1 of 2019 against Port Adelaide – after he had swapped clubs – he went to me again, and again we got smashed. Maybe that established a connection in their mind between close checking me and Melbourne losing. I'm not sure.

I can definitely think of games where it's worked against me though. The Geelong boys – Rhys Stanley and Mark Blicavs – have done it well in some contests, but not always. Adelaide did it a couple of times – making sure someone was standing in front of me, bumping me, getting me off my game – but I think I've gotten them back the past two times we've played. I guess it's a strategy like any other – sometimes it succeeds and sometimes it fails.

When Goody tells us to do it to opponents, I think it works best if there's a real method behind the tactic. A little push and shove in between goals seems useless. I would have thought it was better to do it against me ahead of a marking contest, or while I'm running to make position, but I suppose you risk giving away a free kick in those situations. That kind of niggle isn't really something I love or hate about the game. It's just an interesting thing that happens.

We beat the Power by 31 points, and that felt like a steadying win. Port were a strong and mature side, playing in front of that rabid, parochial crowd, in a big game. It was Thursday night football and we jumped right out the gate. We led by three goals at half-time, but it felt like more – Charlie Dixon had kicked a late one to bring the margin in to 19 points. Petracca was a beast, with 33 possessions and three goals. He had 484 metres gained to half-time alone. But the guy I want to highlight here is Harrison Petty.

Harry Petty won't show up in the coaches' votes, or be listed in the best on ground, but dig a little deeper into the various individual performances that night and he was pivotal. He had 12 touches and seven marks, playing that crucial role as tall defender, taking the second-best key forward the opposition has to offer. That mightn't sound tough, until you consider that the second-best key forward on any team might be Jeremy Cameron or Eric Hipwood, Jack Darling or Jack Riewoldt. Sometimes he takes the best forward, too. Take the Grand Final. If Aaron Naughton had played slightly higher, Petty was going to take him. Naughton ended up playing a little bit deeper, so Steven May played on him, but we were ready to unleash Harry. Goody's got a lot of faith in him.

Harry debuted in 2018, playing one game. We played against St Kilda, and his first disposal was one of those weird kicks where you drop it so badly that it almost rolls down your leg, bumping a few times along the way – it was like he kicked it seven times in the one touch. From memory, he had a one-on-one battle with Josh Battle, and I think he lost that battle. *I just like saying 'Battle'* – and we lost. It was a bad game for the team all round, but Harry was collateral damage and straight away was dropped.

In 2019 we threw him forward briefly because our attack was so depleted. He missed all of 2020 with groin issues. He came on this season after Adam Tomlinson did his knee. But we knew we had a player throughout it all. His body has been a prick to him, but he's 197 centimetres, a young country lad trying to develop, and sometimes it takes the tall boys a while longer than others.

He stepped right in this year and played the role well. And that just gives us so much flexibility. Some back lines play with four tall defenders, and now that we have Tomlinson coming back, and Joel Smith banging down the door, it's easy to see how four out of May, Lever, Tomlinson, Petty and Smith can play in the same side.

Imagine a game in 2022 against Richmond. Tomlinson takes Riewoldt, Petty takes Lynch, Lever does what he does, and that leaves May to take on a match-up like Dustin Martin. If Harry Petty can stand toe-to-toe with big-game forwards, that frees May to curb a Toby Greene or a Jake Stringer or a Jordan De Goey, and that's a big strategic advantage. More than any other line on the footy field, defenders are a group of interlocking parts, fully dependent on one another.

That's why I feel bad about what happened to Harry last season. When we went into the hub last year, Harry was injured, and so he was left at home. He was one of 15 not brought up to Queensland in the initial exodus. He's a good country kid from Wudinna, out Ceduna way, in South Australia, and that's where he stayed, alone. Later, we brought 12 of the others up to the hub, via their own little mini hub on the Gold Coast, but Harry was left at home isolating by himself. And we didn't get in touch with him that much. He reached out to me at the end of the year. He told me – straight up – how it felt. That he felt like no-one cared about him. That he felt left out. That he felt a bit ostracised even.

I'm not sure I saved that situation – I can't claim that credit – but we had a really good chat. It made me realise how someone can slip through the cracks, not feel wanted, feel as though they're on the verge. And when you find that out, it makes you pay attention to the whole list.

It also gave us some lessons about what to do differently. The main thing I took out of it is that I'd take the full 45 guys wherever we're going from now on, no matter what, and that's exactly what we did in the finals hub. We knew that 15 or so of those guys were probably no chance of playing in Perth, but it was so important to keep that group together. It's a cultural thing. We want to be a club that creates the best environment for people to perform, and if you're leaving people behind, that's clearly not the best environment – and that's where we had a miss with Harry.

He's a good kid, with good hands, and he can play at either end of the field, which is an important part of our arsenal. It's up to us to remember that, and remember to make sure he knows we value that, because that's how he came out this year and nailed his best footy. Yeah, he had some bad feelings, but, looking back, that only makes sense. He's someone that really thrives in feeling a sense of belonging, and he didn't have that, but he does now. He absolutely belongs.

CHAPTER 19

Round 18

This was a prick of a game. It was raining, middle of winter, on a Saturday night at the MCG, with no crowd. Having come from that raucous atmosphere at the Adelaide Oval only a week earlier, this was just deflating. I like to say that game day is game day, and I go into every contest with a full head of steam, but then you run out onto the ground on an evening like this and just think, 'Damn, this is really weird.'

It was honestly hard to shake. Going from big crowd to no crowd, dry weather to rainy, and a damp and deserted MCG is about as gloomy as it gets. It's usually a place where there's life and colour in the grandstands, and all this energy from our fans, but on a night like this you're just surrounded by this massive cold steel cauldron. That somehow fed into what happened on the ground, too.

It's strange the way that happens with these games. Games that lack atmosphere so often end up close. No team really gets a run on, because they don't have the crowd and the momentum they bring. It was close at quarter-time and I just knew it was going to be close all night. We got in front in the last quarter, but we blew it, and Luke Breust kicked a really good goal to finish the game off for them. We had some chances. Clayton Oliver kicked the ball to the centre of the ground rather than the pocket, and we had a few misses from Kozzy and Gus.

But the Hawks missed their chances, too. A lot of the statistics on the day looked good for us, but I don't think the numbers tell the story of the game. Goody said the same thing immediately afterward – that the *game itself* told the story, and the story was that Hawthorn were hungrier and worked harder for longer. Our urgency wasn't there. And sometimes when that happens, the siren goes and nobody wins, and you walk off the ground in darkness shaking your head, because that's all you can do after a draw.

One guy who can hold his head up, however, was Jack Viney. He was immense. You could actually see it coming, too, that he was building towards something at this stage of the year. His injured toe wasn't bothering him anymore, and he was charging across the ground again. He had

32 touches against Hawthorn, and 11 tackles, in conditions just meant for a rampaging bull like him.

He started the day off well by getting into the head of the opposition, too. At least we thought he did. Adem Yze had been an assistant coach at Hawthorn, and he suggested to Jack that he should go to Tom Mitchell at the first stoppage and pretend that he was going to run with him for the match. Yze had a feeling that Mitchell might be thrown off his game early if he thought he was going to get tagged. In the end, on Brownlow night, Mitchell got three votes, so I don't think it did very much. Viney got a vote, too, though. It was definitely the start of his surge. At the end of the year he really stepped out as the best version of Jack Viney.

I think he's had time to really grow into himself as a person, and as a father. He's got this great balance in his life now, and he's found his right place at the football club. He's such a great player to play with – you walk out next to him every week and know everything you're going to get. I know people really pump his tyres up over some of the stuff he does, but if you actually sit back and just watch the way he attacks the contest, you can see why people get excited. He's pure. Take his first tackle on Jack Macrae in the Grand Final. *Pure.*

I think that comes back to his leadership. Jack became part of the leadership group in 2016, and he made it clear then that his style would be to 'lead through action'. He became co-captain with Nathan Jones in 2017, and took that role-modelling to a new level. When I was made sole captain in 2020 and Jack was appointed vice, I told him that nothing had changed in my eyes from the year before, when he was captain and I was vice. We knew the names on the badges didn't matter – we were going to lead together, and push the club forward in our own ways.

If he had hurt feelings about losing the title, they didn't show. We caught up about it early, with a chat at Cheeky Monkey in Richmond – *You haven't been part of the footy industry in Melbourne if you haven't caught up for coffee with someone at Cheeky Monkey* – and he said that he wasn't going to hide that he was frustrated with how we were playing, but he also knew the areas that he wanted to develop and grow, and he's gone and done that. I have, too, and we've grown into a really good pair, with great young leaders below us as well, which I think is a brilliant sign for our future.

I know that there was some random talk in the off-season that Geelong had made an offer to bring Jack to the Cats, but I'm assuming that's just part of the game good managers play. It's possible he wasn't getting everything he wanted from Melbourne, and that sort of trade talk can get people's attention. Every footballer – no matter how loyal – needs to put family first at some point, and I'm sure he weighed that up – but I also very much doubt he was ever going to leave Melbourne, especially to Geelong. If you've ever watched him play against Geelong, you will know pretty quickly that he wants to kill them. The day Jack Viney goes to the Cats is the day I pack up my boots.

That's part of the appeal of Jack Viney – this idea that you can set your watch to him. I don't mean necessarily in terms of possessions. There's no linear consistency to the form Vines displays these days. One day he has 30 touches, the next day he has 12, and then he has 30 again, and then he has 20. He's not Clayton Oliver, having 25 to 35 every single week. The important point here is that those numbers might fluctuate, but it doesn't mean Vines is bouncing in and out of form. It's his role changing from week to week, and he just happily goes and does it, whether he's running with an opponent who's hot, or sliding to the half-forward flank for a spell. What does he do? He goes and practises his tackling and grappling for those tagging jobs, and spends extra time on his goalkicking for when he rolls forward.

He knows that James Harmes will want more minutes in the middle, and that James Jordon and Tom Sparrow are going to improve, and that Luke Dunstan has just arrived at the club with his own dreams and ambitions. Jack has finished higher up in the best and fairest more regularly than any player over the past decade, and it's not because he stars every week – it's because he'll happily walk off the ground with 14 disposals and a goal, as long as we all get that win.

I know what Jack Viney looks like from the outside. He's got that scowl, and he leads with his chin, and he looks like a warrior. But the truth is he's still basically 14. He's a big gamer, for instance, absolutely addicted to his gaming. His wife Charlotte is his childhood sweetheart. His daughter Mila is his world. As a man, he's so far removed from that bull on the field. I think he's been able to switch between those sides of himself for a long time, probably since childhood.

He tells this story, about how he was mucking around one day at under 14s training, and his dad, former Melbourne champion Todd Viney, was sitting there in the car watching, and as soon as Jack got in the car after training, his dad roared, 'What the hell was that?' Jack was taught by Todd to play ferocious footy, but that doesn't mean they're ferocious people. Fans confuse the player with the person all too often. Jack is still basically a kid.

He plays for the love of the game, but I wouldn't say he's one of those players who adores everything about the industry or the product. Every 18-year-old loves footy when they get drafted, but the AFL is also not the best landscape for some, and I understand that. I don't watch a lot of footy myself. I can't. I get too frustrated by the simplest things – from the way a team is playing to the stuff the commentators say. At some point I realised all of that was out of my control, so I stopped watching. I think a lot of players – Jack included – are like that.

The alternative is that you keep watching it, and reading it, and listening to it, and it becomes the air you breathe. If it becomes the air you breathe, you can quickly fall out of love, not just with the AFL, but with the game itself. And if you fall out of love with the game itself, you fall out of form pretty quickly, too, and then you fall out of the system. I've seen it happen. As a professional player, I need to reset from time to time. I need to get back to how 15-year-old Max felt about footy, and then shut out everything else.

Jack does that. You can't imagine how well he does that. You wouldn't believe me. He says some hilarious things in meetings – just baffling – but they speak to that life balance that he's found. We'll be sitting there, talking about how a new young player has taken the league by storm – the latest in a long line of young players who take the league by storm. A new one pops up every season, after all. And Vines will chirp up, just amazed at what we're saying about this latest young tyro, unable to understand why we're going to tag this kid called Sam Walsh. He'll genuinely shake his head, and maybe ask 'What number is he?' It's because he hasn't watched footy for three years. He probably thinks Chris Judd still plays for Carlton. He's shut himself off from the game in order to play the game – ignoring footy to stay in love with footy.

CHAPTER 20

Round 19

Saturday July 24, 7:25pm
Melbourne Cricket Ground
Melbourne (9.11.65) versus Western Bulldogs (13.7.85)

When you're playing against a flag contender, you know it. That's true of any season, but it comes into sharper focus when you're in the mix for the premiership, too. When you suspect that your opponent in any given match has the tools to win it all, you pay even more attention to how they use them.

We lost to the Western Bulldogs in Round 19. It was another one of those games at the MCG with no crowd. Again it was wet. The stats make for interesting reading. Interesting in the sense that they're not really conclusive. We had more contested possessions – but were beaten slightly at clearances. We had fewer marks overall – but more marks inside 50. Tackles were about even, as were forward-line entries. They had more one-percenters and more running bounces, certainly more shots on goal and more time in the lead.

But what does all that tell you when the margin is just 20 points? The Doggies even got a few goals late, meaning the scoreline for most of the night was far closer. It might surprise you, but the message I took out of that contest was that our game style would stand up. By which I mean, we were beaten or matched in plenty of key areas, and yet we were still up to our necks in the game.

These are the kinds of things coaches analyse as well, and when they began looking even deeper, they found more things to hearten the playing group. The Dogs kicked a lot of forward-stoppage goals, for instance. Why would we see that as a positive? Because forward-stoppage goals aren't something you spend a lot of time accounting for or worrying about. Some teams might go 10 weeks in a row without conceding a single forward-stoppage goal. Another way of putting it is that forward-stoppage goals aren't a reliable, repeatable source of scoring, and the Dogs kicked five that night.

You can look at that in two ways. You can view it as a source of concern for us – as something that's gone deeply wrong and should trouble the brains trust. Or you can do as we did, and recognise that giving up forward-stoppage goals is not a normal, recurring weakness of ours, meaning with a little planning and tweaking, we'd be able to eliminate or mitigate that problem the next time we met. Imagine the game being played again, exactly the same way, only this time we stem a few of those unlikely goals? Suddenly we win. That's the kind of discovery you can have within a loss – the kind of learning that gives you real belief heading into a rematch, which for us would be heading into a Grand Final.

To me the contest was between two pretty even teams. I always saw us all season long as two even teams. I went into the Grand Final thinking we were two even teams – but with two completely different game styles. Again, that's why these games are so important. You have to understand how they win if you're going to engineer their loss. If you're going to get past them or over them, you have to know how to cut through them. And that requires work, and study, because they are a seriously good football team.

It starts with their hands in close. The Dogs shuffle and give with quick handballs almost as soon as they receive it, making them really hard to tackle. Next, they control the ball moving forward with some elite kicks, and they look hard for targets. That might sound obvious, but some teams don't mind sending the ball back into a contest – backing their ability to win the ball after taking the 'long down-the-line' option – and the Dogs aren't

MAX GAWN - CAPTAIN'S DIARY

one of them. Don't get me wrong, their ability in those contests is strong, but they prefer not to go there – it's their last option.

I suppose if you had Caleb Daniel and Jack Macrae and Marcus Bontempelli in your side, and they had the ball in motion, you would want them to back their obvious skills and look for the lace-out option, too. That's what they do – they catch you off guard and go through the middle, opening up the field with skill. And that speedy ball movement leads to good open looks at leading forwards, and that leads to good scoreboard pressure.

It's hard to say how we were feeling coming out of this game. I can only assume our fans were nervous. Counting back, our form line now read *Loss, Draw, Win, Loss, Win, Bye, Loss*. And yet, so many teams were running through their own rocky patch of the season. Certainly Geelong was flying, but of the other contenders, Port had lost to us, Brisbane had lost to us, and the Dogs had lost two of their previous five. We were in the top four, with four rounds left to play.

I do get nervous though, and it's easy to feel that way late in the year. We were finishing with the Eagles in Perth, and the Cats in Geelong. I'm sure people were doing all sorts of predictive calculations that might see us slip out of the four. It's natural, particularly when you see a strong unit firing on all cylinders.

Bontempelli had 31 touches and two goals – he's so scary when he gets the ball forward of centre. The coalface ability of Liberatore was there again, with 27 touches and six clearances. Jack Macrae (38 disposals) and Caleb Daniel (34 disposals) were so significant – they always are. The marking of Aaron Naughton gives you a headache, and from a ruck point of view the work rate from Tim English always keeps me moving. Bailey Smith had 26 possessions, nine tackles, and nailed a shot on the run just before half-time to put them 21 points in front. We had only kicked 2.7 – our lowest half-time total of the season.

But again, all those individual performances provide that little bit of motivation and intelligence – fuel for the next time you meet. It's important to take as many notes as you can. I'm sure that game helped Steven May against Naughton. I'm sure it helped Ben Brown against Alex Keath. I'm sure Viney would have learned from playing on Libba, and Clarry would have picked up something from watching Bont, and Langdon the same with Smith. Because their weapons were on show that night at the MCG, just as our weapons had been on show at Marvel.

Goody always said to us that the team that improves most throughout the year would be the team that wins it all. The team that we were in Round 3, or Round 6, or Round 9 – or Round 19 – probably wouldn't have won in September. You need all the losses and all the wins from the season to come together, before you understand what you're made of. That's what we did. We learned about their delivery inside 50. We learned how dominance in hit-outs doesn't lead to dominance at clearances. We learned to look at everything, and take stock, and put all the lessons into practice.

We didn't know it yet, but there were seven games left in our season. We were about to win them all.

CHAPTER 21

Round 20

Sunday August 1, 12:10pm
Marvel Stadium
Gold Coast (4.6.30) versus Melbourne (18.20.128)

The season turned in the strangest way in this round. Although, I guess we should have been used to strange by now. We were supposed to play the Suns on the Gold Coast, which seemed like a simple enough thing given how well Queensland had done avoiding COVID outbreaks in 2021. But it wasn't simple at all. Melbourne was in lockdown, and so from midday on Thursday all players, coaches and staff had to isolate for 48 hours. We could only leave our homes to get a COVID test, and to train on Friday afternoon. Some of the guys isolated in hotel quarantine, and I believe it was nicer than it sounds – they were staying at the Sofitel. I stayed home. So far, so normal.

On Saturday, game day, we arrived at the Melbourne Jet Base, ready for a 9 am charter flight for our 3.20 pm game. Even that was a little odd, having the plane to ourselves and only one person per row. An hour into the trip, things went off course, literally and figuratively. A flight attendant came up to me: 'Excuse me, are you Mr Gawn?'

He wanted to speak to me at the front of the plane, and I immediately assumed I had been to a Tier 1 site. 'I've just been in contact with the AFL,' he said. 'They've called the plane and they want to know if you want to turn around – if you want to land in Brisbane, or turn back to Melbourne?' Firstly, I said, 'None of the above – I'd like to go to the Gold Coast as we were planning.' But that wasn't an option anymore. I also said, 'I'm really not the guy you should be talking to. As much as I'm sitting in seat 1A and I'm the captain of the team, I'm not the captain of this flight, and I think you probably want to be talking to someone down the back.'

I sent our general manager football operations, Daniel McPherson, up to the front, and then we quickly learned that Queensland was going into a pretty quick snap lockdown, and that was happening around 5 pm, so we probably wouldn't be able to play. We landed in Brisbane in the end, and we stayed on the plane for about three hours.

We knew we were playing in Perth the following week, and would need to quarantine for a week when we got there, so now the flight attendant – who was by this point my new best friend – explained how there was a chance the game against the Suns would be abandoned, and we would fly immediately to Western Australia. All this time, of course, we were just sitting in our seats on the runway.

People started getting hungry, and the dinner we were going to eat post-game was sent for and delivered to Brisbane Airport. I think it took them an hour to drive more than 50 poke bowls up to us. Christian Salem must be picky, because he ordered something different from Uber Eats, and the driver literally came up to the fence beside the plane. The pilot got out to go and grab this Uber Eats bag from over the fence.

We got an update later, which was met with a groan. 'This is your captain speaking. We've had a change of plans. We will now be heading to Canberra to refuel before flying to Perth.' That turned out to be a lie. We really should have recognised the voice. It wasn't the pilot – it was Christian Petracca, who was now apparently on good enough terms with the cockpit staff to commandeer the intercom.

Eventually, we learned that we would be flying back to Melbourne. People immediately got into game mode, doing stretches up and down the plane and drinking water. We arrived back in Victoria at 4.30 pm, after eight hours of travel, and we would be playing the Suns at Marvel

Stadium the next day. I had left my house at 7 am and got home at 7 pm – and I quickly remembered how tired and sluggish I was after all the travel to reach Tasmania and play North Melbourne earlier in the season, which I took onboard. I wasn't going to let that get to me again. I made sure to get as much sleep as possible – to relax and not do anything that might cost me crucial energy the next day. I went for a little jog around the block, even though it was 8 pm and raining, but it helped me get centred and ready.

In some ways Gold Coast might have had things worse. They would have been looking forward to playing in front of their fans, in the warmth and humidity, and instead they had to get on a plane unexpectedly, get COVID tests, sleep in a hotel, then get up early for a random 12.10 pm game in chilly Melbourne, at Marvel Stadium with no fans, knowing their stay might not be for a weekend but potentially for longer, in a hub situation in the middle of a Melbourne winter.

We won by 98 points. That might sound meaningless – thrashing a side that's already near the bottom of the ladder, that's injured and young and come through a long season, then had their preparation disrupted and their home advantage taken away. But delivering a performance like that, at that time of year, can be crucial going into finals. Knowing what it feels like to win big and score heavily and get on a run is the kind of thing that sets you up for a tilt at a flag. Richmond beat Fremantle by 104 points in Round 22 of 2017, on the way to their drought-breaker. Having a big win shows you what fluent football looks like, and reminds you what you're capable of doing when everything clicks.

Between the 26-minute mark of the first quarter and the 20-minute mark of the final quarter the Suns didn't kick a goal. Meanwhile Petracca, Oliver and Harmes were having a field day. I got involved, kicking a couple of goals, including a rare banana. Amazing to think that this strangely delayed game, which ended in a 16-goal rout, was Jake Bowey's debut.

Jake travelled for 12 hours the day prior, as did we all, only he was thinking about his first game, about how he was going to play against the Suns in front of a crowd. He probably arranged tickets for a few people he knew on the Gold Coast, and then suddenly he was back in Melbourne, playing in front of no-one. If it was a crazy weekend for me, I can't imagine what it was like for Jake.

He did well though. People were making comparisons with Caleb Daniel after his first half, in which he had 11 touches and was running at 100 per cent efficiency. He almost pulled down a screamer in the third quarter – playing at this level must have seemed easy. Still, you would have been hard pressed to convince him that he was about to win seven games straight, and become the fourth player in history to win a premiership before losing a single match.

But the guy I want to talk about here is Luke Jackson. He was nominated for the Rising Star Award earlier in the season, and of course he ended up winning the entire thing, but I think we all too easily forget that external people were doubting him a little at this stage of the year, questioning his place in the side, and whether he could really maximise that second ruck role. But this is the game where he confirmed everything. He kicked four, had 17 touches and was in everything. I really began to feel like I could trust him – that whatever I threw at him he would go and do. I had Jacko run around in the ruck and he took care of it, with 13 hit-outs and a few clearances, but he also slid forward and hit the scoreboard.

Jacko is only two years into his career, and I already feel like it's the best ruck–forward combo I've been a part of. My weaknesses are his strengths, and vice-versa, so we have this relationship where we cover for each other but also drive one another. My strength is my ruck work and my marking and my reading of the game, and his strength is his follow-up and his speed and agility on the ground. I can't learn speed and agility, but I feel like I've gotten better in my follow-up, in my ability to clear the ball and join in with the midfielders – while his marking and ruckwork has improved out of sight.

He's from the suburbs of Perth, and could have been a national basketballer. He played Under 18s for Australia. He's actually not the only guy on our list with that kind of talent, either. Joel Smith got to that level. Christian Petracca, too. Corey Maynard was on our list for a while, and he was with the Cairns Taipans briefly. It's funny though, if you listened to the commentators, the only guy in the AFL with a basketball background is Scott Pendlebury. It's part of footy folklore – *Pendles played hoops* – along with the fact that I smoked a cigarette once on the way to training. But honestly, I've heard basketball writers say that Jacko and Petracca and Smith might all have played with the Boomers at the Tokyo Olympics if they had chosen that path instead of footy.

Second-year rucks aren't supposed to be as good as Jacko. I always thought that was a myth, about big men maturing so slowly. Look at guys like Tim English and Sam Draper and Sean Darcy. But then I think about it more deeply, and those guys are 22 or 23. Jacko was tearing up the field earlier this season when he was 19. In some ways I think he's this new-age player, in that he wants to play every game possible and play at a high level, and won't let anything stop him from that, least of all some perception about the limitations of being young and tall.

He's a unique character though. Absolutely hilarious. In the nicest possible way. He was paired up with Nathan

Jones on his first camp, and Nathan likes to teach the kids a thing or two about reality, but Jonesy had no idea what he was up against with Jacko. I remember Jonesy coming to me afterwards, explaining how Jacko had told him that he had never heard of a pineapple. I don't mean pineapple as in slang for a $50 bill or something like that. Jacko had never heard of the fruit. He'd never heard of pineapples. I'm not sure how that's possible.

And he really does say some stuff that is ... odd. In the hub in Queensland last year, we were training one day – literally in the middle of a session – and Jacko stopped in the middle of the drill. He stopped moving, and started looking off into the middle distance. I asked him: 'What's up, mate? What's the problem?' And he just kept staring, and he goes: 'What are we doing here?' I told him that we were training, it's a bloody full ground drill, and we should probably get back to that. And he goes, 'Nah, I'm talking bigger picture – what are we doing on Earth? The signs are pretty clear that this planet is cooked – shouldn't we be out finding another planet?' I was amazed – gobsmacked really. 'Shut up, Jacko,' I said.

ROUND 18: DRAW

Hawthorn, who were hovering around the bottom of the ladder, hung on for a disappointing draw. Jack Viney fought hard with 32 touches and 11 tackles (10 the week before).

ROUND 19: LOSS

James Harmes gave his best against Tom Liberatore, but the Western Bulldogs beat us by 20 points, never letting up. This was a team we knew we needed to learn to conquer. Needless to say, this was to be our last loss for the season.

ROUND 20: WIN

COVID-19 wreaked absolute havoc with a flight to the Gold Coast that went nowhere and we ended up back in Melbourne playing at Marvel Stadium the next day. Regardless, we played some great footy against the Gold Coast Suns and Jake Bowey made his debut.

ROUND 21: WIN

We were at the pointy end of the season and it was our first outing against West Coast in Perth, who had been unpredictable most of the season. It was a close match but we won it by nine points. Alex Neal-Bullen starred with two goals.

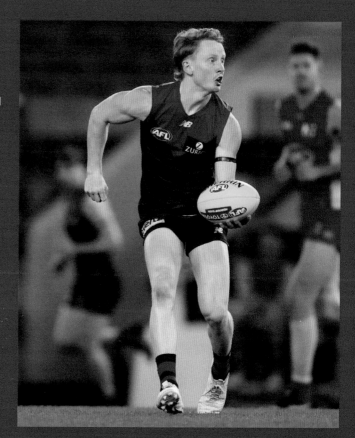

ROUND 22: WIN

We seemed to have found our form after a mid-season slump and nailed the Crows with a 41-point win. Bayley Fritsch kicked seven goals straight, including the last three of the game – a goal haul that he would come close to repeating in the Grand Final.

ROUND 23: WIN

Geelong came for a fight and led at three-quarter time 12.3 to our 6.7, but against the odds we turned the game around in the last quarter and my goal after the siren cemented our place at the top of the ladder. We won by four points.

QUALIFYING FINAL: WIN

Brisbane were the highest-scoring side in the competition and we were entering a finals campaign with a team that had virtually no finals experience. Our 30-point lead at half-time meant we never looked back.

RIGHT: Luke Jackson, who won the AFL Rising Star award, takes a high-flying mark.

BELOW: Steven May challenges Lion Lincoln McCarthy for the ball.

PRELIMINARY FINAL: WIN

With our confidence buoyed by the previous win, we hit Geelong with everything we had and won by 83 points to demolish any thoughts the Cats had of knocking us out. The Grand Final awaited us.

ABOVE: The teams line up before the Preliminary Final in Perth.

LEFT: Angus Brayshaw kicks a goal.

GRAND FINAL

The intensity was being felt by all the team as we walked out onto the ground in Perth. This was our big moment. The Western Bulldogs were not going to give up without a massive fight.

FACING PAGE TOP: The team photo before the final.

MIDDLE: Christian Salem is tackled by Bailey Smith, Marcus Bontempelli tackles Harrison Petty.

BOTTOM: Clayton Oliver celebrates a goal.

THIS PAGE TOP: Jack Viney takes the ball from Tom Liberatore.

MIDDLE: Jack Lever shrugs off a tackle from Cody Weightman.

BOTTOM: Tom Sparrow gets the ball away.

TOP LEFT: Christian Petracca is named the Norm Smith Medallist.

TOP RIGHT: Celebrating with the fans.

MIDDLE: Our coach, Simon Goodwin, gets into the celebrations.

BOTTOM: The team gathers for a winning photo.

CHAPTER 22

Round 21

Monday August 9, 6:10pm

Optus Stadium

West Coast (9.9.63) versus Melbourne (10.12.72)

Recovery is so important after a game. You can't imagine the structure that goes into repairing bruised bodies immediately after matches. The importance of stretching, and strapping, and icing, and eating, and hydrating are all drilled into you as a new recruit, until the process of warming down and staying mobile – yet somehow also resting and recuperating – becomes second nature.

Nowhere in that guided system does it recommend that you head immediately to the airport and get on a four-and-a-half-hour flight, squeezed in a seat that's too small, before finding your way to an unfamiliar hotel. But in season 2021, immediately after our win against Gold Coast, that's what happened. It was Sunday, and we would be playing the Eagles in Perth the following Monday after seven days of quarantine in Western Australia.

This became another sliding-door moment for Nathan Jones, too. We took only 30 players to Perth, and most of those who stayed behind believed there would be a VFL match to play. Jonesy had played only a half in the VFL the week earlier, so rather than come to Perth only to be an emergency, he stayed in Victoria, deciding that he would put his best foot forward by getting a full VFL match under his belt.

Then Melbourne's outbreak grew worse, and the VFL was cancelled. Worse still, while he was at home digesting that news, Jack Viney got suspended, and so one of the guys who had come west with us – Aaron vandenBerg – came into the side against the Eagles as the medical sub. It's fair to say that if Chunk had been with us in Perth, he could have been the medical sub.

In another twist, we used the medical sub less than any club in 2021, but when Jayden Hunt injured his ankle early against the Eagles, this became one of those times when the sub was used. VandenBerg played the majority of the game and he well and truly deserved to be on the ground, but it's easy to imagine an alternative reality where Jones gets on that plane with us, comes across, is named medical sub, then gets on the ground and plays three quarters of wet-weather footy, and stays in the team for the rest of the season. That's COVID though – crazy.

The craziness was apparent the moment we landed, too. I remember looking out the window and wondering if there were fugitives on the loose. There were cops *everywhere* at the airport – coming onto the plane, just outside the plane, escorting us by road. It felt like a police state. Funnily enough, once we were at the hotel, I didn't see another policeman for the rest of the trip. There was no-one stationed at the exit of the Mercure. They just gave you this one warning: 'If you walk out that front door, it's an immediate $50,000 fine.'

We stayed there for three days, and then, oddly enough, we changed hotels, switching to Joondalup Resort. The Western Bulldogs were playing Fremantle, and it wasn't fair for one team to be stuck in a city hotel while the other could stretch their legs at a more spacious resort, so both teams were given half a week of each. Once that was all done and it was game day, at least all the craziness was over. At least, I thought it was.

The game started well enough. We got to a point where we were as comfortable as you can be in a football game with a full away crowd – up by four goals with 17 minutes to go in the last quarter. Petracca (28 disposals and six clearances) and Oliver (28 disposals and nine clearances) were firing, while Ben Brown kicked three goals and

Jackson (21 touches) continued to show his talent. But the torrential rain brought something else with it – lightning.

James Harmes reckons he actually saw lightning, which is disturbing, because it suggests he wasn't exactly looking the right way. Either way, we suddenly had to come off the ground. Everyone was annoyed but I was slightly relieved – if lightning *was* really coming, then it was probably coming for all 208 centimetres of me.

We were told we would be off the ground for 20 minutes, which turned into 30 minutes, and then we were back, and so were the Eagles. Before we came off, I was starting to get into my groove. I felt like I had used my running to good effect, to finally get the better of Nic Naitanui. Then a force of nature gave him a rest, and he came out all guns blazing. I remember he took a mark and kicked a goal and almost won them the game. We've had some good battles, and that turned into one. He's got such a massive frame. People underestimate his strength and size. They think his rucking is about athleticism and jumping at centre bounces, but he's equally powerful at ball-ups and throw-ins, so you don't really get an easy look anywhere against him.

I like to think I can match his strengths, and that most ruck contests between us end up as a draw, with the ball at our feet, but his work in the middle of the ground is better than mine. And then when you have that full crowd behind him, and they get a sniff, and they come back into the equation, he just goes to another level. You feel pretty guilty when that happens, and you can see Clayton Oliver trying to hold on to Tim Kelly for dear life because he knows Nic Nat's just going to put it down his throat. He's a class act, so I'll call the night a draw and just say I'm looking forward to a few more battles in our early thirties.

The Eagles had trailed by 33 points at one stage, and they closed to within nine points with 80 seconds to go. But we won, and pushed the Bulldogs out of top spot on the ladder. Xavier Ellis interviewed me immediately after the game and said, 'Did you take any learnings from the lightning break, in terms of what you could do better for next time?' I almost started laughing. 'Mate, I'm not going to write down *anything* to do in my next lightning-interrupted match,' I told him. 'We may another day have to come off the ground for 30 minutes, halfway through the final quarter of a match, but honestly, I'll take the chance that's not bloody likely to happen again.'

The player whose performance I think was overlooked in this game was the guy we call 'Nibbler'. Alex Neal-Bullen had a cracking game. Simon Goodwin had told media in the lead-up to the match – knowing the forecast – that we were keen to play 'groundball', making use of the conditions and keeping the ball on the deck, and that suited Nibbler to a tee. He had 20 touches, eight tackles and two goals.

This is a guy who got better and better and better and better throughout the whole year. He got voted into the leadership group at the start of the year, too, which from an external point of view might have surprised a few people, but within the club he's just so well regarded for his standards and his habits and his work rate and his selflessness.

If that doesn't compute, I understand why. Nibbler was put up for trade only a year ago. The 2020 season had been frustrating for him. He was injured, and at one point was suspended for a month for a sling tackle, all of which meant he only played seven games. He ended up staying with the club, and you might imagine he'd be disgruntled about being offered up around the league. On the contrary; he appreciated the honesty. He wanted to stay, and he did, and he took everything he heard from our coaches and put it into his off-season preparation.

What had let him down sometimes – by his own admission – was his polish. And so he went away and worked on that to a crazy level, where now he's become one of our better inside-50 kicks.

His role requires him to run incredible distances at speed. He's one of those athletes who can do repeat high-energy sprints all game long, until he's tallied up some outrageous number like 16 kilometres covered. What he needed to add to that was precise first-option kicking.

And that's what he's done – he came out and played 25 trademark games, combining his talent in time trials with his obvious football talent as a junior. He's 25 now and it feels like everything has clicked for him. He's easily one of our first picked every week. He's become a leader, too, in that 'team within a team' of pressure forwards: Nibbler and Kozzy and Spargo and Chandler and Jones.

Spargo is learning a lot from him in particular. Spargo is a guy who gets 11 touches a week, but those touches are perfect. He lowers the eyes, looks for a target, and hits it – every time. I didn't see that coming – his creativity – because he's such a fit little bugger, and competitive, too. He and Neville Jetta would get into a scrap every bloody intraclub match. They would play on each other, and end up fighting, both sharing that white-line fever – but also a cool football brain. He's become a weapon. Put it this way, if the opposition put their best small defender on Kozzy, and their fittest on Nibbler, they don't have much left for Spargs, and that's when he becomes dangerous – 18 goals for the season is a nice little return for a pressure forward. Nibbler's taken these young guys with him in more ways than one. In 2021 no AFL player had more tackles inside 50 than Alex Neal-Bullen. Number 2 on that list? Kysaiah Pickett.

Still, I think the thing Nibbler will be most proud of – beyond his consistency and leadership and, of course, that premiership medal – is the way he identified a weakness and turned it into a strength. It's one of the hardest things to do in football – to admit a shortcoming, and work on it – because the work is frustrating and it might never turn for you. Not everyone can kick with the skill demanded at the level. The advantage Nibbler had, I think, is that he knew the skill was there. Deep down he always had it. He just had to bring it out of himself – to get some confidence back.

He could always kick a footy, but kicking a footy in that part of the ground is a different beast. Midfielders get some grace, some permission to blast out of a stoppage, to be inefficient. But when you're playing high half-forward as Nibbler does, you don't get many cheap and easy disposals. He has to work his arse off for every touch, and when he gets one he's probably fatigued. He's probably under extreme pressure, too, and his opponent knows exactly where he wants to kick, and the person he's kicking to is under more pressure again. It's the hardest kick in football. If you can nail that option – *and not everyone can* – it becomes a lever the team can pull. You don't win flags without guys like Nibbler.

CHAPTER 23

Round 22

Sunday August 15, 2:10pm

Melbourne Cricket Ground

Melbourne (16.8.104) versus Adelaide (9.9.63)

T he scoreline says we beat the Crows by 41 points, which
makes it sound like a one-sided contest between a team
on top of the ladder and a team near the bottom – but
that's not how it was. This was a close game. A tough
game. And another bloody game at the MCG in front of
no crowd.

This time it was Adelaide's turn to isolate on their way
into our state, although we also had to retreat indoors for
a couple of days as well, in order to meet South Australia's
strict contact rules. We actually had to do a COVID test
early on the morning of the game, and it meant we got to
the ground long before the first bounce – at around 10 am
for a 2.10 pm start.

That might have been a major inconvenience in our preparation – the kind of thing that sometimes knocks me off kilter a little – but I ended up doing a wonderful thing that otherwise I'd never get to do. I got to sit on the grass at the MCG for an hour before the game. I just sat on the wing, by myself. It was a beautiful day. A real spring day. And I took in what time of year it was, and how finals were coming, and why this game mattered – why it was important to close out the season well and finish on top.

It was a good moment, and then the game happened, and that was filled with not-so-good moments. I was up against a second-gamer, Kieran Strachan, the type of assignment that I said before I tend to struggle with, and sure enough he had a dozen touches and 25 hit-outs. Their on-ballers were all over us early. It felt like Paul Seedsman had 20 bloody touches in the first quarter alone. Ben Keays was dominating. Rory Laird was on top. Honestly, it felt like we had our heads up our arses, the same as the last time we met the Crows. They came after Clayton and Christian in terms of contact in the midfield. It was a brutal contest.

We were missing Tom McDonald up forward, and playing Ben Brown and Jake Melksham as our talls, which wasn't quite working. And even when we moved it forward, we sent it there poorly. The sun was out, so it looked like a beautiful day, but it was windy – really gusty – and we just couldn't control the ball cleanly. It looked for a while like an upset was on the cards. The Crows booted four of the first five goals of the third quarter, and closed within three points.

But we finished strongly. It was a win. We were able to stretch out and flex a little at the end, and we cracked that little hoodoo we had created for ourselves – of losing at the MCG without a crowd. We were in a great position to attack the following week for a shot at the minor premiership. A large part of that comes with thanks, of course, to Bayley Fritsch. Bailey kicked seven goals for us that day, including our last five. His last three came in the last three minutes – the final one kicked on the final siren.

It's been an interesting journey for him. He's this lad from Coldstream, which conjures an image of some nuggety kid playing biting winter footy out in the low-lying chill of the Yarra Valley. But of course he's not that. He's slender, light, and a stylish aerialist. The way he launches at the ball is almost artful. He plays with a kind of grace.

Yet his path hasn't been smooth, or particularly linear. He was taken by us as a mature-age player in the 2017 draft, and debuted the following season. Bayley played every game in 2018, except one. He was dropped for the preliminary final. I'm not involved in selection, but I think he had been slightly out of form in our previous two finals, and we might also have gotten a bit spooked by the big West Coast forwards. The Eagles were so exceptional in the air that season. Bayley was playing on the wing back then, too – he wasn't yet an attacking target – so we went with a tall defender, Joel Smith, to help combat Kennedy and Darling and Allen and their resting ruckman. I don't think it ended up mattering a lot to the result.

Funnily enough, Bayley now finds himself as part of a similarly tall forward line – as the fourth marking option after Tom McDonald, Ben Brown and Luke Jackson. He's just under 190 centimetres, so his primary role is bringing his tackling and his leaping. He's almost that handy hybrid player you find in all successful teams, like Josh Caddy was for Richmond, or Liam Ryan is for the Eagles. It's someone who can mark the footy or halve contests but be dangerous at ground level. If he gets a small defender, he'll dominate him in the air. If he gets a tall opponent, he can work them over on the ground. Inevitably, there are going to be days where he kicks a bag. He had six goals against North Melbourne earlier in the season, six in the Grand Final, and seven on this afternoon in Melbourne.

He seems a natural in the position. I know that's actually caused Simon Goodwin to question why he ever tried making Bayley into a wingman, or experimented with him in defence, despite his potential for intercept marking. 'I was an idiot to do that,' Goody admitted on TV one night. 'I don't know why I did that.' He's every bit of a forward. That's obvious now.

Bayley is now a leader in our forward line. On Captain's Day in 2019 I tipped him to win the Coleman Medal, and everyone sort of laughed at me – and to be fair he got nowhere near it that year. But this year, after counting all his goals in the finals, only one player kicked more than him, Geelong's Tom Hawkins. And Bayley had the fifth-most marks in the league inside 50.

Part of the reason he's improved so much is his goalkicking, which again you have to trace back to the patience of Greg Stafford in helping every player develop his own routine. Last year Bailey kicked 22 goals and 24 behinds. This year he kicked 59 goals and 24 behinds. To add 37 scoring shots – and for every single one of those added scoring shots to be a goal – is a pretty outrageous change.

I don't know what he says or does or thinks when he composes himself for a shot, but I do know that he and Ben Brown are out there practising their shots longer than anyone else. They're the two that work on it the most – kicking in that extra 30 minutes every session – and they're the two that have been able to reap the most reward.

I've always loved watching Bayley play. He played for the Casey Scorpions, so we saw more of him than most of the league would have. He always looked that little bit skinny, that little bit undersized, and you always worried a little bit about whether he could do what he did at VFL level in an AFL match. But there was also a fierceness that was obvious about him, too, if you watched closely. There was a game out at Casey Fields shortly before we drafted him, and I was paying attention, and you knew then that he could play – that he wouldn't be overawed.

I remember he was clearing out the forward 50, completely, just with his voice. We had all these other talls down there, guys with experience and guys with promise – like Sam Weideman. But Bailey knew he was the best option to take the grab at that moment, so he got rid of them all, and cleared out his space. He was like, 'Get out. It's my 50. I'll take it.' And he did.

CHAPTER 24

Round 23

Saturday August 21, 7:25pm

GMHBA Stadium

Geelong (12.5.77) versus Melbourne (12.9.81)

To properly understand Round 23 of the 2021 season – Demons versus Cats, down at Geelong – you need to go back a decade. I don't want to dwell too long on that day every Melbourne fan knows – *Round 19, 2011, when we lost by 30 goals* – but unfortunately that's where the story starts. You need context, and context in this case is 'The 186ing'. That losing margin is etched in the memory of all the Demon faithful. Our reserves lost that day, too, by 120 points – adding up to a 306-point capitulation by the club as a whole.

I didn't actually play that day in either game. I was the carryover emergency, with Clint Bartram. It was eerie to watch it all from the grandstands, and worse to feel it in the rooms afterwards. I remember driving home with Jack Watts, Jack Trengove and Luke Tapscott. There wasn't a word spoken for the first 45 minutes.

Clubs move on quickly after most losses, but not this one. There was one peculiar stab at normality, when champion runner Steve Moneghetti randomly came in and spoke to the playing group the next day. It had been scheduled in advance, so they kept the appointment despite the thrashing. I can't remotely recall what he said to our stunned mugs. A day later, Dean Bailey was sacked as coach, and Todd Viney took charge. In Viney's first game as coach the next week against Carlton, both Bartram and I played, I guess because not taking part in either loss made us the most in-form players on the list. That was obviously a really bad low. As low as they come.

In 2015 there was another notable chapter in our history. It was Round 12 and Corey Enright was playing his 300th game, and we spoiled the party, winning by four goals, breaking a longstanding losing streak against them at that ground. I also remember beginning to find my feet as a player. There was a late withdrawal of a Geelong ruck – maybe Trent West or Mark Blake – which meant I would be going up as first ruck against a forward in Josh Walker (who was undersized), and a utility in Mark Blicavs (who hadn't yet done much rucking). I had 44 hit-outs, 19 possessions, eight marks and a goal – my breakout game. I got interviewed afterwards – my first on-camera post-match interview – and I got asked how I felt after taking those first few marks. I said 'invincible', and the next day Paul Roos – who never stood for that kind of nonsense – had changed my magnet to 'Mr. Invincible'.

In 2016 we added another chapter to the feud. It was Round 23, and we had just botched an outside chance of making the finals by losing to Carlton in Round 22. We had no finals hopes left coming into the final round, were probably feeling sore and sorry for ourselves, and although I felt like I had a good game and a good year – my first as an All Australian – we went down to the Cattery and got bulldozed. It was a disaster. We lost by 111 points in Roosy's last game as coach.

The history of animosity only continued to build in 2017. We played the Cats in Round 3 at Docklands. I tore my hamstring off the bone and was out for 10 weeks. We lost by 29 points, but it was far closer than that. We were within a kick in the third quarter, and fights were breaking out everywhere. It was a heated, spiteful game, and I've always thought of it as the real catalyst for this rivalry we've had with Geelong.

Things went to another level again in 2018. Round 1 at the MCG, I missed a shot on goal to put us in front with 30 seconds left, and we lost, and again it was heated. Later that year, in Round 18, we blew a four-goal lead at

Kardinia Park. I've never seen Neville Jetta be out-marked, but Zach Tuohy – who's a defender – goes down and takes an unbelievable grab on him, and then kicks a goal after the siren to win them the game. As if the drama wasn't done for the season, we played the Cats in an elimination final. Nathan Jones was the hero, with a goal at the start of the fourth quarter. Mitch Hannan also did that massive run down the wing to kick a goal, and suddenly we've won our first final in years in front of 91,767 fans.

If that wasn't crazy enough, fast forward to 2019, and a Round 2 match-up. It was Steven May's first game for the club. At the time I thought it was the weirdest game of footy I'd been involved in. We dominated the play – had all these disposals, contested possessions, inside-50s – and we lost by 40 points. It was bizarre.

In 2020 Adam Tomlinson missed a winning goal just before the end of the game – again with that soulless feeling of a game at the MCG with no crowd – and Geelong triumphed by three points. And that brings us up to speed, up to the final round of the 2021 home-and-away season, again against the Cats, again down at Geelong. They're firing, we're firing, and all that history is behind us. Like I said, context.

Most players drive down the highway to get to the game, but I didn't. Because I live on the Mornington Peninsula, I decided to take the ferry from Sorrento to Queenscliff.

It was a risky move, since I get seasick. I checked with the AFL Players Association whether I was allowed, and apparently that was fine. We're not allowed to catch public transport during COVID outbreaks, but the ferry got the nod. There was one condition – I had to stay in my car. There were only three cars, when there are usually 100. A few fans tried to get me to open my window for a chat, but I couldn't even do that. I had to mime 'Sorry' to them. I hope they understood.

You know the story of the way this game begins. Geelong touched us up. Badly. But I do remember getting into the rooms at half-time and learning that the numbers weren't actually that bad. We were doing fine in most key areas. The problem was that the Cats had pounced with goals directly from centre bounces. Those are hard to counter, and they're also deflating – they suck the air out of you. Rhys Stanley is one of the hardest rucks to stop when his confidence is high, and he was definitely up. Dangerfield was hot, too, and so was Selwood. Gary Rohan booted a goal 20 minutes into the third quarter, and they were 44 points in front.

All we did to change things was put on our hard hats and got to work, chipping away, doing nothing special but everything essential. We got a few goals, and that felt good. We played with a little freedom, and got some centre-bounce goals of our own, and that felt better. We came out in the last quarter and got the lead back with 12 minutes to play, and that felt amazing. Momentum is a funny thing. We had simplified our centre bounces, and everything clicked. And that's another lesson we took going forward. There was a point in each of our three finals – against the Lions, the Cats and the Dogs – where we referred to those centre-bounce goals Geelong had scored, and how we would be able to get our own, and how getting your own shifts everything back your way. The fact that we won against Geelong in Round 23 was hugely significant, but arguably more so was the self-belief we earned by turning momentum on its head.

That self-belief had been building, and becomes obvious if you look at the last month or more of the season in isolation. We learned how to pile on a score swiftly, playing forward-half football. Hitting the scoreboard heavily against Gold Coast helped. Needing only one quarter to turn the game against Adelaide from a close one into a 41-point victory was useful, too. Before those games, we were losing to the Dogs with a score of 65, or beating Essendon with 68. We were playing low-scoring matches, so to be able to play football that could rip apart a final meant everything to our confidence.

We should go through the last part of the game though, because when else will I get to relive the detail of the greatest comeback in club history?

Geelong were in front with two minutes to go, and they were chipping it around, which they're good at, trying to ice the game. Angus Brayshaw tried to soccer a loose ball off the ground, but it skewed over the boundary line, and a free kick for insufficient intent was paid against us. I was surprised by the call – I'd actually set myself up for a throw-in. Cam Guthrie, an experienced Cats midfielder, took the kick, and somehow put it out on the full. Two key things happened next.

The first is that a Geelong player spoiled the ball with two fists, despite it being over the line, and his spoil sent the Sherrin 10 rows deep into the empty stands. A 50-metre penalty was paid against him for time-wasting. The second and little-known element? A Melbourne physio named Brenton Egglestone clearly realised how important it was to get the game moving quickly again, and so he vaulted the fence, dived into the right row and immediately got the ball into the arms of Jake Lever. That bit of clear thinking meant everything – because it cost the Geelong defence crucial seconds to set themselves up.

With 27 seconds to go, Lever was ready to take his kick, and we exchanged a look. I love it when I can lock eyes on the kicker. In that instant we knew he would kick to my advantage, but we just as quickly looked away, down at the ground, so we wouldn't give it away to the opposition. He sent it forward to the hot spot, I took a double grab mark, and got to line up for goal with scores 77 to 75 in their favour. A goal to win.

My first thought? 'Why do I do this to myself?'

My second was to recognise that everyone was telling me *not* to rush, and the siren sounding really helped with that, because I was *definitely* going to rush. I heard a lot of the other noises around me after that. I heard the heckling from the Cats. I was copping an absolute barrage, mostly about my miss in 2018, when the ball barely hit my foot. Harry Petty and Jake Lever must have had similar fears, because they couldn't look at me, or the kick. They literally faced in the opposite direction.

Brayshaw came up and said, 'Don't listen to anyone Gawny, you've got this.' Maysy ran up and told me, 'I'll love you no matter what.' And I felt like I could hear Greg Stafford encouraging me through my goalkicking routine, making sure I didn't go too far with my natural arc. I put it through, and was just buried in teammates.

It was the first time in club history that we've won a game after the siren. For the first time in 56 years, we were the minor premiers. People questioned the outpouring of emotion, because apparently some pundits have got nothing better to do than question players celebrating 44-points in a back-from-the-dead victory against a fierce rival going into an historic finals series. I was more than happy to celebrate that win. If you can't go nuts when something like that happens in footy, why bother playing at all.

After that win – after that home-and-away season – the Melbourne supporters were up and about. The lid was off. My mum opened a bottle of wine after the game, which she never does. My phone blew up. Funny man Hamish Blake sent a congratulatory text. Fellow funny man Ryan Shelton sent a video.

There was one person I didn't expect a congratulatory text from, and that's my father-in-law, Lyle, a mad Geelong supporter. It runs deep with him. His other son-in-law is James Frawley, and I'm reliably told that James received a frosty reception throughout Hawthorn's entire premiership era. I love that kind of passion.

In the 2018 Demons–Cats game, when Tuohy kicked the goal after the siren to win, I had been getting booed the whole game, I think because people thought I had staged for a free kick. I later learned that my father-in-law was booing me as well. Suffice to say that he didn't want to talk to me after I kicked that goal. I sent him a text the next day asking, 'Why haven't you sent me a text?' and he goes, 'Just getting over it … we'll beat you in the finals.'

When we got to the Preliminary Final this year against the Cats, my wife, Jess, asked him, 'So who are you going for in the prelim?' And he goes, 'It'd be really nice to see Joel Selwood win one as captain.' And Jess goes,

'Your bloody son-in-law is the captain of the other team! Wouldn't it be nice to see *him* win one as captain?'

He was still going for Geelong all the way through that prelim. Jess watched it with her mum, and Lyle watched it by himself. They tried to call him at half-time, but he wasn't talking to them. They tried to call him at three-quarter time, and he got angry. When we won, he said he didn't want to talk to me for a few days. And that's what footy is about, because if it doesn't mean everything, maybe it means nothing.

Lyle did finally send me a text though. It was a photo of him wearing a Demons scarf, and a short but excellent message: 'Looks like I'm going for Melbourne in the Grand Final.'

CHAPTER 25

Qualifying Final

Saturday August 28, 7:30pm
Adelaide Oval
Melbourne (13.15.93) versus Brisbane (9.6.60)

We got a whole floor to ourselves at the hotel in Adelaide. We had already done two days of isolation in Melbourne, but South Australia was taking no chances. Each player had a separate room at the ibis for one night of quarantine, and they're not the biggest rooms, so the walls began to close in on us early on Friday night. We had to wait seemingly forever for dinner, but it arrived a little after 9 pm. There was a knock at the door, and everyone on the whole floor opened their doors at once, stuck their head out into the hallway, and found a tray of food on the floor. The staff were like ninjas – we never even saw them.

We weren't allowed out of our rooms until breakfast, at which point we could eat together in a common room.

Then we were funnelled onto a bus and driven to Adelaide Oval for a mid-morning team walk. That was quite good – an hour of throwing the frisbee, tossing a few spirals with an NFL ball – the whole playing surface to ourselves. Then we went back to the hotel and stayed until game time. We got our warnings about that, too: no going to the fence to touch fans, no taking the ball back from the crowd, either – a sanitised Sherrin would be provided instead. There were photos of stadium staff spraying down the goal posts with disinfectant.

My previous experience of finals has always been sudden death. And that gave those matches an entirely different feel. But because this was a Qualifying Final – because we had the double chance – this felt more like a game we were there to win, rather than survive. It was a chance to enhance our position within the season, rather than save it, and that meant something for our confidence.

Simon Goodwin probably didn't get a lot of press this season, at least in comparison to what a few other coaches in the league received, and he probably likes it that way. But he still has that instinct to be a storyteller, to inspire with messages. The messages that night were two-fold, and they were themes he had built throughout the season.

The first example he called on from international sport was Andre Agassi. Agassi famously hated tennis – finding it a laborious, painful grind – but he had a mindful method for winning. He went into any tournament knowing that he didn't have to be the best player in the world – he only had to be the best player on the day itself. He needed to beat his opponent, then move on to the next opponent, and the next. By focusing only on his immediate goal, he found his way to the ultimate goal. That was a great maxim for us, but it wasn't the one that truly connected with the group. Remember that most of this team are millennials – they've never seen Agassi play, or probably even read his stunning autobiography, *Open*. Maybe they needed something more modern, and Goody gave it to them.

His second theme was a philosophy only just this year explained by the NBA Finals MVP star Milwaukee Bucks forward Giannis Antetokounmpo. The 'Greek Freak' riffed on a similar idea – the importance of resetting within games, within weeks, within seasons. He delivered a drought-breaking NBA Championship for the Bucks this year, and people began to listen to his explanations. Everything for him was about staying in the present, and never being satisfied.

We watched videos of him speaking to media, and he put everything so well. If you think too much about all the great scores you've put up – the triple doubles and perimeter domination – you're going to play poorly in the days that follow. You're going to be terrible. 'When you focus on the past, that's your ego,' he said. 'When you focus on the future, that's your pride.' Antetokounmpo focused instead on the present – on the moment. 'That's humility. That's going out there and competing at a high level, and enjoying the game,' he said. 'That's the skill I've tried to perfect, and master. It's been working so far, so I'm not going to stop.'

Now, I can't pronounce his name, but what he told the world really resonated with us. A bunch of our players really love the NBA, and I think that's why this clicked for the team. You could see the gears ticking over in everyone's mind: 'This guy is the best basketball player in the world right now, and he doesn't give a shit what's just happened or what comes next. It's all about the now.' We had never been in this position before, so being distracted by possibilities could have derailed us, but we had his truth ringing in our ears: Let's not worry about last week, or next week, or the Grand Final. Let's worry about literally this moment right now – this Brisbane game.

Strategically, we had to consider a few things. Their down-the-line set-up is strong. Their forward surge is strong. Their intercept game is strong. They have tall forwards who dominate. They have midfielders who kick goals. As a contest, it felt that it was like for like.

Preparing for that, we looked at how we had played against them in Round 12, when we won by 22. We looked at how they had just played against West Coast in Round 23, scoring 125 points. We looked back at our match against the Cats only days earlier, about what we did wrong and right.

We had an advantage when the Qualifying Final started and more as it went on. Eric Hipwood was now out with a long-term knee injury. His replacement, Dan McStay, was injured early in the game, leaving Joe Daniher isolated. Those kinds of seismic shifts in the availability of your tallest players can have a big impact.

But they weren't about to lie down. Charlie Cameron kicked five against us – he was on fire. Lachie Neale had 46 touches. Still, they were behind by 30 points at half-time. And then came the most important quarter. The Lions dominated us in the third – they absolutely had their way with general play. We kicked only two measly points for the entire term. Importantly, though, they only kicked two goals.

It felt like we had restored part of the game to the way we wanted it played. After all, Brisbane had kicked 26 points in the first quarter. Multiply that by four, and it equals 104 points for the game – and no team had managed 100 points against us all season. The important shift was that after that bad start, Brisbane only kicked five goals in the next three quarters. I remember how hard it seemed for them to score.

Our midfield was moving well. Oliver had 33 touches, seven clearances and a goal. Alex Neal-Bullen had 27, plus five tackles. The Lions closed in on us in the final term, only for Petracca to deliver us two goals within a minute – a death blow. But it was our defence that stood up. Not just Jake Lever and his 15 intercept possessions – it was the entire side.

It's worth mentioning Troy Chaplin here. He works directly with our defenders as a line coach, but he's also responsible for team defence more generally. He came to us in late 2016, after retiring as a player at Richmond. It's a pretty tough progression to go straight from playing into coaching – I've seen a lot of guys attempt it in my 12 years, and they often come in and go straight out again. He kept learning though, keeping himself open and vulnerable to new lessons and wisdom. He has that willingness to improve.

He's extroverted, which always helps as a coach – particularly seeing as Goody is quite naturally introverted. He presents to the group often, where Goody is the classic senior coach delegating and watching. It's great to see the things he's been trying to implement with us for five years take effect. It must be rewarding for him.

I think it's evidence, too, of the fact that you need to build a team up slowly, establishing all your key pillars, embedding trust, baking in all that understanding, and that takes time.

There's a stereotype about premiership sides, that you need this five-year slow burn, where most of the pieces on the chessboard are in an ideal demographic – the right age (mid 20s), with the right experience (more than 100 games) – and it feels like we've hit that sweet spot. We've matured enough to take on all the solid defensive habits Chappy has been trying to instil. And when that happens? You stop the best attacks in the AFL in their tracks.

The siren went, and I was over the moon. I finished on the bench with May, Lever and Petracca. They like me to get a 10-minute rest if they can. It was amazing to soak it all in, do a lap of honour thanking the Melbourne fans in Adelaide. In the rooms it was a nice feeling, but also a feeling of knowing that we had another one to come. The other half of the playing group was already in Perth waiting for us, watching from a hotel. It felt like the start of something, and I guess it was.

It was the start of being away from family again. We were two days into what became a month away from home. And I remembered that when we first got to Maroochydore for the hub in 2020, it was that first week when people missed their family the most. Melbourne was feeling the pain of lockdown, too, so stresses were high.

We left Adelaide the next day, to start our two-week quarantine in Western Australia ahead of the Preliminary Final. We wouldn't emerge from it until the day of the game, two weeks later. The players were given the week off, and we tried to treat it that way, not talking too much about the match we had just played, and not at all about the one coming up.

Goody was so strong and stable and calm through all of that. And it started immediately after that win. He spoke in the rooms about how proud he was of our defensive efforts, how every game from now on was a new season, how we should all use our time to centre ourselves best, by relaxing, or zoning out. Now was not the time to focus and think. I got back to the hotel that night and felt completely calm. I had a glass of red, went to bed early, woke up, got on the plane, and didn't talk footy for a week.

CHAPTER 26
Hublife 2.0

We already knew Joondalup Resort quite well – from the best common areas, to where to go for a stroll, to the staff themselves. The coffee was good, which is a blessing. It felt comfortable being back, albeit straight into quarantine, knowing we would all be there for two weeks together, with no-one coming or going.

But we were at a loss trying to stay entertained. People do go a little stir crazy. I think Goody walked up to 1000 laps of the car park. Then there was the board game crew. Sam Weideman, Tom McDonald, Jake Lever, Jake Bowey, Steven May and I played Settlers of Catan. Ben Brown introduced everyone to a board game based on Game of Thrones. Little pockets broke out quick Monopoly Deal contests. Neville Jetta, Toby Bedford and Kozzy Pickett – had a card game going. I don't think they were playing Texas Hold 'em though – probably Asshole. You do what you do to pass the time.

You found your way into certain rhythms. I had a cup of tea in Adam Tomlinson's room every night for four weeks. I'm not sure if I was invited by the end of it, but we did it anyway. Alex Neal-Bullen and Jake Lever would join us to watch the conclusion of *Australian Survivor*. When that finished, we jumped on *SAS: Australia*.

Brekkie was generally at 6.30 am, lunch around noon, dinner at 6 pm, but there was a little bit of flexibility – sometimes a lot. Trent Rivers and Luke Jackson are the ones who like to sleep in. They could stay in bed until midday if you let them, and in that first week we did. I can't do that. I go to bed early and rise early, too, so the placement of my room probably wasn't ideal.

Joel Smith's room was on one side, and Clayton Oliver's on the other. If you wanted peace and quiet, and selected rooms in order of tranquility, theirs would be the last two. You didn't want to be anywhere near them. Joel would open his door and you would quickly find James Harmes, Bayley Fritsch and Mitch Brown hanging around, playing PlayStation or watching a movie. Then there was Clayton on the other side, with Harry Petty, Kade Chandler and James Jordon in there with him every single day. There was so much dumb noise coming from those rooms.

Luckily, I can sleep through pretty much anything. If it had been anyone else in the room next to those boys sitting up giggling and gaming until midnight, they would have cracked the shits and told them to shut up on day one. I just closed my eyes and waited for the sun.

We were actually allowed to get out and enjoy the sun a little in that first week, too. It sounds odd – being given permission to get out into the sunshine – but you do need to control your exposure to the elements. In the first week it didn't matter, but in the week approaching the game, too much sun can easily dehydrate you, or make you fatigued. Sunburn tires you out. But in that first week off, everyone hit the pool.

When we got back into training, in week two, we went to a few different places. We got on a bus and went to train on the oval of WAFL team West Perth. We did our main session at Optus Stadium. We even trained on the oval of the West Coast Eagles. The West Coast facility is unbelievable – I've never seen anything better in my life. The Casey Oval is really, really good and Gosch's Paddock is getting redone and will be really, really good, too, but you look at what West Coast has and you realise that there is a facilities gap. Not that it matters. It's more about the group and the environment you create within those facilities. We've got one of the ultimate does-not-want-to-drive-anywhere people in Ed Langdon. He loves his Fitzroy, doesn't want to be in his car, wants to walk to training, but he commutes out to Casey and he's happy as Larry.

If he's happy, it means we've created a solid environment, even if the perpetual roadworks on the Monash Freeway make it a shocking trip.

The two weeks in the resort reminded me of that, in that the circumstances weren't ideal, but we made the best of them, and we created a really great place that people wanted to be. Staff were hanging out with players, and players were hanging out with staff. There were all the cards and games and video games. We had an NBA 2K tournament on the PlayStation. Jonesy and I partnered up, just to see if we could play, and we beat Luke Jackson and Trent Rivers, who were the favourites.

We had a trivia night. The smartest Demon is Angus Brayshaw, by a country mile. I think he scored quite a high ENTER ranking in school, but he's also street smart. His trivia brain is next to none, especially in music.

Of course, the fun and games don't last forever. Eventually Monday rolled around, and our opposition coach, Sammy Radford, drilled us on what Geelong were going to bring. Once upon a time Sammy was a high-level under 19s footballer, and later a high school teacher. He also played with the Sandringham Zebras during their famous run of three premierships – under Mark Williams. He coached with Luke Beveridge at St Bedes, Mentone, then he coached our VFL boys at Casey, and then he joined our oppo team. He watches a *lot* of footy.

He'll present to the coaches before he presents to us, and then together they come up with what they present to the players. A coaches' oppo meeting might go for five hours, while a players' oppo meeting goes for 10 minutes. I've sat in on the coaches' version before, and you look at everything they're trying to digest, and you realise you can't tell the players all that – their heads will explode. I remember one time being present when they dissected an opponent for half a day, and telling the players, 'Boys, get ready for this oppo meeting, because it's a doozy.' We went into the auditorium and they had condensed the whole thing into five slides.

The opposition coach is a funny role though, because really, their general message is to play the way we've been playing all year. We're not going to tinker too much, especially at the end of the season. Sammy always picks out a few statistics that might highlight strengths or weaknesses. He does have a problem though, in that there's one particular statistic – *Defensive 50 Groundballs* – that he likes to tell us about all the time. Every single team we come up against apparently has a D50 groundball problem.

I think I understand it though. He knows that poor performance on D50 groundballs is often a function of the pressure our forwards apply, so he highlights it, knowing our small forwards will be licking their lips and ready to tackle and harass and corral. It's part of any coach's arsenal – telling players what they need to hear most.

Geelong likes to control the ball. We knew that, so we knew our ability to shut down their short kicks would be critical. We also thought we had a height advantage in our forward line, so getting it there quickly would be pivotal. They're obviously good at clearances, with Dangerfield and Selwood and Duncan and Guthrie, so we knew we needed to get on the front foot with Petracca and Oliver, and throw in a few different players they might not see coming, whether James Harmes or Tom Sparrow.

Players were also individually looking at their opposition, too. I even looked back one week, to the Brisbane game, to check my own form. Oscar McInerney had done something different at centre bounces, coming in a couple of steps past the centre line, dominating the airspace – and I found that felt quite awkward. So I tried to develop a counter, in case Rhys Stanley tried something similar. That's the thing – I had to anticipate that Stanley would be looking at recent vision of me, to see what might work for him.

We're all studying one another, after all. We're all thinking about one another. We're all hoping we have the edge. Then we just have to hope it all works together for us on the night. Best-laid plans don't always come to fruition. I think Stanley won the first four contests against me when the game actually started. At some point, after all the rest and study, you just have to trust in yourself and your mates.

CHAPTER 27

Preliminary Final

Friday September 10, 5:50pm

Optus Stadium

Melbourne (19.11.125) versus Geelong (6.6.42)

We played in a preliminary final in 2018, but straight away I could sense a different feeling within myself this year. In 2018 I was probably thinking, 'Oh, we're in a prelim,' whereas in 2021 my mind was saying, 'We're in a prelim to win a granny.' It was completely different. We were happy to be there in 2018. We had just won two finals at the MCG. We were doing that difficult run from fifth, and we were all excited to be in Perth, but West Coast hit us in that first quarter and we couldn't get back. This time we were up against an arch rival – or what I think of as an arch rival, I don't know what the Geelong players think – but it's a history that's been building between us. Looking back now, I was more nervous for this game than I was for the granny.

I think the fans are more nervous in preliminary finals, too. You're just so desperate to be involved in Grand Final week. Not getting that chance at a flag after coming this far is unthinkable. But, then again, if you lose a grand final – from what I've heard – you would rather have lost a week earlier.

Standing on the ground, I felt deeply in the moment. There were 58,599 people there, a full house, with lots of Melbourne fans. I looked around when everyone stood up to sing the national anthem, and it seemed amazing – just surreal – to see a whole stadium full of people rise to their feet at once. We hadn't experienced a big crowd since the Anzac Day Eve game in Round 5. After all those strange, melancholy games played in front of no-one, we had been hanging out for that visceral crowd experience. I wasn't expecting the sea of red and blue, either, but there it was, and we lapped it up.

As we sang 'Advance Australia Fair', we grouped up. We like to do that, get body on body with one another, arm in arm ready to play. I remember looking across at Geelong, and they were standing apart. I noticed a little bit of tape on them – I don't know if that means anything. I'm sure it doesn't. But I just thought about how they had done it the harder way, losing their first final, then playing a second slog against GWS in Perth. We were rested. 'We need to hit them early,' I thought. 'We need to get on top of them quickly.'

And that's what we did. We just got onto a really good start in that first quarter, with five goals to one. That continued in the second quarter, even if the scoreline says both teams added four goals. There was something about seeing Ben Brown mark them early, and Tommy McDonald clunking them, too. I don't know what it is about the big blokes, but when they're flying and taking strong marks, it just gets you into a mindset that you're not going to be beaten.

At the start of half-time, we always take 5 or 10 minutes to compose ourselves. We're still talking, but we're also taking it easy. A few little things might get raised, but basically we're waiting for Adem Yze to share whatever message he has for the group. It's about being calm in the moment. And that's come from the Collingwood loss.

In that game, we came in and we were *frantic* at half-time. We were talking and talking and talking, and we went around in circles, and just gradually got into a worse and worse space. After that, we've always come in at half-time and just taken a big, deep, slow breath. We refocus, rethink, reset – like the Greek Freak. You do what you need to do to get yourself ready, then go to Yze and on to Goody, and then head back out.

We had a 30-point lead, but that's not a safe margin, so we came out after half-time with a point to prove. The Cats had kicked a few late goals – both from centre bounces –

so I had to talk to the mids about that. It felt as though the way we were playing all over the field – especially the way we were setting the ground up – meant that the only way the Cats could get on top of us in the contest was through centre-bounce goals. That meant our little group had a pretty big role to play in the third and fourth quarters.

I kicked a few goals that night. Five, in fact. My most ever, and I'm told the most ever by a Melbourne captain in a final. My favourite one had already happened, in the second quarter. A kick came forward, which I thought was touched off the boot. No-one else thought it was touched – including the umpire – but I had already decided to play on, and snapped it across my body. I try them in training all the time, and belly the ball every single time, putting it sky high, or out on the full, or both. That was a fun goal.

I started to feel really good in the middle, too. I had done a lot of ruck craft study with Greg Stafford during the week. We were watching clips of my footwork post-stoppage with Oscar McInerney against the Lions, and some of it – my ability to spread quickly – was looking really good. We both realised it was something I had begun learning from Luke Jackson. Some of my best games for using my feet immediately after the centre bounce had come in the last month. The important thing is to make sure you're not just watching – that you're actually joining in, not falling over, not standing still, and that you're getting some power into your first three steps after the contest. All of that just gets you involved.

It paid off in the third quarter. The ball was bounced, I rucked well, and then I kept my width well – spreading to the outside – and before I knew it I was running into space, Petracca handballed to me, and then within a few steps forward I was able to let a long bomb go from 55 metres, and she sailed through. We were absolutely on. I was lucky enough to get another goal from a free kick against Esava Ratugolea, and kicked truly. In a contest in the pocket with Mark Blicavs, I plucked it out of the ruck and snapped the goal as I was falling. Trent Rivers speared a kick to the hot spot 20 metres out not long after, and I double-clunked the mark and nailed the shot. All of a sudden I had four goals for the quarter.

People ask me if that's the best quarter I've played, or the best game I've played. But honestly, if I go to my best game ever, there's a Hawthorn game back in 2016 that always comes to mind first. I had 16 touches and five tackles that day, as well as a goal, which doesn't sound remarkable. I remember it fondly because I took 11 marks, nine of them were contested – and I always put big, difficult marks ahead of goals. Funny fact: when I missed the goal against the Cats in 2018 and we lost the game, I was of course devastated to lose, but I was also pissed off because it took the shine off the mark I'd taken to earn the shot. I loved that I had put myself in that position to win, and taken the grab, and I still *hate* having wasted that opportunity.

I took only five marks against the Cats in this final, and they weren't amazing grabs, so when I came off the ground I didn't realise what was going to come my way in terms of media and fanfare. Everyone was just roaring, but I'm sitting there thinking, 'Geez, I left a few marks out there.'

The most exciting part of my game – for me – is that two of my goals were from stoppages, telling me everything I need to know about how I'm learning from Jacko, about footwork and mobility. It's showing me something I can go away and work on and add to my game. Maybe I'm not just a marking player anymore. Maybe I can be someone who can be damaging around stoppages as well. It's great when you're 30 years old but can still see a potential path for improvement.

We kicked eight goals straight in the third quarter, and led by 78 at three-quarter time. What was that like – to be in the middle of that kind of momentum surge? I've mentioned how bad it feels to be on the other side of those centre-bounce goals. In that 2018 Geelong game at Kardinia Park in Round 23, when the Cats were sweeping it out of the middle, you felt so hopeless. The backs were looking at us like, 'Can you *please* put some bloody pressure on?' But when you're on the other end of that dominance, what I've learned is that it's important not to start showboating or trying extraordinary things. You keep doing what's been working, and I think everything we did that night was stock standard Melbourne centre-bounce stuff: relatively normal hit zones, clean first possession, and scooting forward from there. That's Plan A. And Plan A was working.

Around the ground, I thought everyone had a spring in their step. After the third quarter, everyone came back out and was feeling what I was feeling. We were getting to the Grand Final. We wanted it badly, so it felt like once we had them in a position to keep going, we kept going. Everyone joined in. Bayley Fritsch joined in. Petracca was himself. Jack Viney played one of his best games of the year. Steven May went down, which was scary. Everyone was a bit worried about that, then he came back on and everyone stopped worrying.

It's funny how long it takes before you feel in control though. I kept looking at the scoreboard, waiting for something to dawn on me – as if we needed to be 10 goals in front of them to be assured of a win. It just felt like we had to keep going – that there was some chance they would come back. You always sense that, and to be fair, they still had plenty of inside 50s, they still had shots on goal, they still won centre bounces, so they still challenged us in all parts of the game.

I got a chance at one point to kick a sixth goal. As I was lining up, a 'Gawny! Gawny! Gawny!' chant went around the crowd, and it threw me *way* off. I kicked it out on the full, which was good, because if I was going to miss, I wanted to miss everything – kick five straight, without a blemish.

I sat on the bench for the final 15 minutes of the game, which always annoys me. Something I've always loved is being able to get one over on my opponent, so that the next time I play him, he remembers. You want to leave that impression as deeply as possible, but I guess I understand that coming off, resting, not getting injured, is of greater importance than leaving something in your opponent's memory bank for next year. And it was amazing to sit back and see that sea of red and blue cheering. The Mexican wave was fun. I still can't believe we won by 83 points.

Friends and family would have made the occasion better, but they wouldn't have been out there right then, when the siren went, in the middle of the ground. I was interviewed by Abbey Holmes straight after the game, and I remember that as that was happening, all our players were out on the ground – all the non-playing players, I mean. They sprinted onto the surface and began hugging everyone in a jumper. I understand the role I have to do in terms of media, but I'm genuinely shattered I missed that initial hug. Still, I got out there, and grabbed hold of all those guys who played and all those who didn't – all 45 of us together as one. I don't say this lightly: that's the best moment I've had in footy.

That moment really made it clear how unlucky so many of our squad were this season. Most Grand Final sides, you look at them and go, 'There's the guy who was really stiff to miss out.' There's always a player who was dropped two weeks earlier after a great year, or the one who had an injury the week before the decider. The history of football is littered with examples. Every year every team has one or two. If you look at this team, to me, there's so many more than that. There's more than half a dozen hard-luck Demons.

Jayden Hunt is at the top of the list. He played 20 games this season. He had a brilliant year. If any little thing had changed whatsoever in the positions he's versatile enough to play – if the match-ups had gone differently, or a new look was needed – he would have been the first picked.

I remember hugging Adam Tomlinson, who was crying, because he's a crier. Tommo was locked into our defence earlier in the season, but did his knee, and knew he wouldn't be there.

I remember hugging Nathan Jones. Chunk was out there just ecstatic for everyone. The guy is a warrior, a man of such high character, who set the club up to be in this position. He went through two weeks in quarantine, his mind is filled with questions about whether there might be injuries or form changes that would see him play, but he had twins on the way, and knew he would be flying home the next day to be at their birth.

Nev Jetta was out there, fully fit. He's a guy who could easily have done the job required in the backline, but you couldn't wipe the smile off his face.

Joel Smith would have been a chance to take over from Steven May, if May's hamstring had been too serious to risk, but Smith had his own issue, tweaking his own hamstring only days earlier. That's bad luck upon bad luck.

And then there were guys like Melksham and Weideman, hard-luck stories in another way, because they happened to be out of the side in a year without continuous VFL action, and therefore little chance to press their claims.

There were guys people wouldn't immediately think of, too, but who were no less capable of being part of the Grand Final side.

I think of a guy like Aaron vandenBerg, who stayed injury-free the whole season – which is a massive thing for him – who did amazing things in the cultural space with our young players, and who was almost 'best on' for every VFL game he played, and every training session he did. We had a scratch match in between the Preliminary Final and the Grand Final, and Simon Goodwin named vandenBerg the Chris Judd of that session. He trained so well he almost got a Grand Final game off the back of it.

Unfortunately he was behind a few of the best midfielders in the competition.

The other forgotten man is Majak Daw. Majak had an incredible season as a ruckman, too. In every AFL team, the primary ruckmen have had time off with injury at some point this year – except me and Luke Jackson, meaning Majak has landed at the one club where no opportunity to play presented itself. There was maybe one moment where Luke Jackson had played a few quiet games, and Majak was a chance to come in and play in that second ruck and key forward role – then Jacko kicked four goals against Gold Coast and continued shining for the rest of the year. Every Monday we list our 'trademark' players – the ones whose performances were clear and consistent with our values. Majak won that a handful of times for his VFL form. He put together an amazing season. It's not something people talk about often, but you begin to feel a fair bit of guilt keeping a guy like that out of the side, because he has all the tools. In that same session where vandenBerg starred, Majak was all over me. Yes, I kicked five goals in the prelim final – but Majak took me to school in the scratch match, kicking three against me and teaching me a little lesson. I'm excited for what he can bring next year. He's my age. We're both 30 now. And Majak has taught me so much simply by how competitive he is with his training, how much he brings to every session. He's made me a better player, which I'm sure wasn't the main thing he wanted to do this season. He wanted to get in front of me. I hope he gets his chance.

Clubs always talk about depth of players driving competition, lifting standards, demanding excellence – the rising tide that lifts all boats. I think all of those guys played a part, ensuring we were switched on and improving and firing at the end of the season, too. I've always been a big believer that the team that's in form come September tends to be the team that goes all the way. It's felt that way over the past handful of years, whether with the Doggies or the Eagles or the Tigers. Now it felt like it was our turn to take the form and ride it all the way.

I didn't get much sleep that night. I'm a big tennis fan, so I stayed up and watched the US Open. Daniil Medvedev was playing the young Canadian, Felix Auger-Aliassime. I woke early the next morning and watched Novak Djokovic against the rising German Alexander Zverev. It's what I do. I can't sleep that well after most big night games, so I turn to sport, maybe catching a few Mitchell Starc deliveries, or better yet, a climbing stage finish in the Tour de France.

Once I got up, though, I dipped into my phone the morning after and got to see all that celebration from Melbourne fans back home, which was wonderful. Our media team did everything they could to bring the experience back to everyone in Victoria, but it couldn't substitute for a penultimate game at the MCG.

I found myself scrolling through all the messages and tributes, really diving into what the win meant. Someone later asked me about whether I was doing what I could to block that out, focus on the process, and not get caught up in the historical significance of the moment. But I've been caught up in the history of this club since I got drafted. And unfortunately a big part of that history is that the fans haven't been able to taste success since 1964. I knew we had to go one more time, one more win, to break that drought.

I'm a history nuffie. And we hadn't changed history yet.

CHAPTER 28

Grand Final Week

The day after the Preliminary Final, I got up early, got into my car, and headed immediately to the ocean – a place called Waterman's Bay. I forget what the cafe was called, but I just sat there with Ed Langdon and Jake Lever and Christian Petracca, having a coffee and a little breakfast. We must have spent five hours there. I guess that's the way you celebrate finally escaping quarantine – by sitting at a cafe for half the day.

After that, of course, we had another two weeks before the Grand Final, and I didn't know exactly how to play that out. I liked how we had worked things in the lead-up to the Geelong game, but this was completely different because now we were all free. Honestly, I wanted a similar formula, but people had friends and family everywhere, we suddenly had cars, too, and now there were options beyond board games – *and beyond the resort itself* – for killing time. It was actually a stressful first week for me, because I really just wanted everyone to stay at the hotel. I would have loved to have been in quarantine for the full four weeks.

But I also worked out pretty quickly that this is what everyone would do if they were in Melbourne, so it was fine. Everything's fine. I should go and enjoy my life as well, which I did. Many of the boys played golf, particularly the boys who probably weren't going to be playing in the Grand Final. I'm pretty sure Mitch Brown played a round every single day. Then there were the surfers – James Harmes was always catching waves. I was one of the cafe boys, keen to grab breakfast with anyone who was interested, or dinner that night, sometimes both with the same people. I like the camaraderie of shared meals. But there were also people who seemed to know everyone in Perth. Michael Hibberd must have been out seeing a friend every night. Angus Brayshaw was the same.

Our head of communications and media, Clare Pettyfor, set up a day for media to come in and chat. She's quite tough, so while in previous years during finals we've sort of said, 'Hi everyone, all media – come on in and do whatever you want', Clare had a tougher approach this year, keeping it contained to one day for photos and interviews. We weren't the only team they were talking to, naturally, but the Doggies were in quarantine that whole first week that we were out, because they were coming from a Preliminary Final in South Australia against Port Adelaide, so they still had a week of confinement. That almost made us the main show in town.

The second week, most guys got a break, and media was mainly me and Goody. I have two regular radio gigs throughout the year, with RSN and Nova, both of which I did. I also did a New Zealand radio show, and then did a local Perth one with Adam Gilchrist. I did AFL360 on the Wednesday night, and then Captain's Day on the Friday. None of it was too stressful.

We still had training sessions, of course, which kind of drew you all back together. We had an intraclub scratch match, too. By the time the Monday of Grand Final Week rolled around, we all began to gravitate back to one another naturally. We didn't need to make any rules about people staying at the hotel. We just found that everyone – the 23 who would be playing, in particular – gradually started eating at the hotel more, having breakfast together, having dinner together. We had all these Zoom commitments, keeping in touch with past players and sponsors and board members. It was busy, in a great way.

We had the Brownlow Medal night, too, which was unique. It was at Optus Stadium, and the Doggies were in one room and we were in another room – everyone else was in a main room. Bizarrely, we got to see Doggies players in the shared toilets. I remember running into Josh Dunkley there. 'Hey, mate' – 'Hi, mate.' I'm not big on small talk with footballers at the best of times, let alone against a member of the team you're about to play in a grand final when in the toilet of the Brownlow Medal ceremony. We did really well though, in that Clayton Oliver finished third. Marcus Bontempelli came second, so they did well as well. Both teams are probably happy that they actually didn't have the winner, because the media would have been crazy for that week. To be fair, Clayton might not have been happy to miss out, but we were fine. He can win it one year in Melbourne if he wants.

I spoke to a few former premiership players during the week about what to expect coming into the Grand Final. Jordan Lewis was succinct: 'Lap it all up.' James Frawley was the opposite: 'You can pull back and say no to stuff, if you want.' Chris Dawes was quite funny: 'During the game, surround yourself with good players, so shit players like you will get a medal.' That was a great quote, and in fairness, I have surrounded myself with the best midfield going around, with Oliver, Petracca and Viney. I took all of that advice onboard, but I was always going to do it my own way. I've done everything my own way since I started, and my way is that I'm happy doing media. I'm happy being out there. I'm happy being in a busy cafe, getting a muffin and a coffee and saying g'day to the barista. I'm an extrovert. I just don't find those interactions stressful.

I wasn't stressed, either, about being favourites, because I don't even check that sort of thing. In my mind, we had played the Bulldogs three times in 2021. They got hold of us in the pre-season. We beat them at Marvel. They repaid us at the MCG. They had a 2-1 lead, but this was a different game, different circumstances, different conditions. I was pretty carefree about predictions, happy just knowing that it was going to be a good game.

We had a main training session back at Optus Stadium. The Western Bulldogs got to train there first, we were second. Luke Jackson and myself have been doing an hour of early ruck craft all year long, so we arrived early, along with Greg Stafford and Jake Lever, who comes to help out, and Clayton Oliver, who uses the time to work on his hands. That's when we noticed the Doggies were training. We didn't go and watch. I just respected their privacy. But the Western Bulldogs watched us train, which was funny. Actually, I think there's a ripping photo of Luke Beveridge peeking over a fence. It didn't bother us, but when our whole squad was training, the Bulldogs players were definitely standing in the race, watching us, almost like they were trying to show their presence.

There wasn't much I needed to do as captain to settle the group in that final week, although I did keep a close eye on things. I love observing anyway. I'm a big people watcher. I also know my 45 teammates well, and feel as though I can tell how things are going for them. I'd seen red flags in the Queensland hub in 2020, so I knew what to watch out for – how this person might be susceptible to being away from family, or that person doesn't like being around the boys too much. Honestly, I thought everyone did it well, the way they handled themselves.

There were definitely nerves creeping in towards the end, but coaches quash that well, making jokes here and there, slipping something funny into a presentation. A guy like Christian Petracca is an unbelievable source of energy, and a great person to bring everything up or down a notch as required. Steven May was probably the one causing some concern, as he obviously had a strained hammy, and you could tell he was nervous, so you had to comfort him – but you also just always knew that he was playing. He probably didn't play his best game, and he certainly felt his hammy at times, but he did have a six-centimetre tear in the muscle. His opponent, Aaron Naughton, ended up kicking just the one goal, and that one was almost shared with Harry Petty – it's another good lesson in trusting a player to know his own body.

The whole week was set up well, and then we came to our final meeting. The Captain's Run is the generic term for it, but we call it Demon Day. Because it was an away game, we did it at night, 5.30 pm. It's a big meeting, everyone knows this. But someone was late. The time comes, and Angus Brayshaw is nowhere to be seen and no-one knows where he is. Then we called him and he goes, 'I forgot.' He forgot about the Grand Final Captain's Run – he forgot about Demon Day, before a chance at a premiership. He was with his brother 20 minutes down the road. Goody was cool and calm, and just goes, 'We'll wait 20 minutes.'

Now, when things like this used to happen, it would end with some form of group punishment, like, 'We're all jumping off the Port Melbourne pier tomorrow at 6 am.'

And that used to happen a bit. Ever since I've been captain, we've done a more compact punishment: a two-minute plank. And nothing was going to stop us just because it was the Grand Final the next day. So we all did a two-minute plank, all of us clothed, in the dinner room, because Angus was late. It was actually pretty funny, and set the mood up perfectly.

The meeting had a special touch. Goody had told us to bring our headphones. And then during the meeting we all got an email, with a personalised three-minute video, highlighting vision of each player throughout the year. All 23 of us sat in a circle, watching ourselves, set to music, bringing the very best of what we brought all season, and what the coach wanted us to bring the next day.

Everything and everyone just felt .... normal. Perhaps it was because we had been there for almost a month, or that we had been there before, but it seemed as though we had created a home away from home, a safe and relaxed environment. The only thing that unsettled me was my dinner the night before the Grand Final. The chef came out – and we hadn't really spoken during the hub – and he presented me with this dish: 'I made you these special meatballs.' I started to wonder if he was a Western Bulldogs supporter, and what was in them, because he seriously came out with three *gigantic* meatballs and said: 'These are for you, captain!' They tasted great. I felt fine. But it certainly caught me off guard.

The hub environment does tend to knock you off your usual pre-game rituals, so I stuck as closely as possible to the new ones I had created there. I kept the nightly cup of tea thing going, visiting Adam Tomlinson's room with Jake Lever for a cup of English Breakfast. I usually have a bowl of cereal before going to sleep the night before a game, so I did that, too, although I did change it up slightly, going for Crispix instead of Weet-Bix. And the final ritual I kept going was the first thing I did when I woke up.

Since the hub began, I had gone to the beach every morning at 6.30 am. Usually Jake Lever came, and Christian Petracca, as well as our fitness coach Selwyn Griffiths and Tom Sparrow. I actually had a bit of hammy tightness in the two weeks before the Grand Final, so the salt water soaking felt therapeutic.

On the day of the Grand Final, it was just me and Jake Lever. We headed to our little spot at the same time as always – 6.30 am – and jumped in the water. The beach was called Mullaloo, and it was bliss. The beaches in Western Australia are something else. I mean, you have to dodge sharks, but they're beautiful. If we were in Melbourne, we would be standing there waist deep – Speedos on the bottom, hoodies up top – but here I was swimming. Actually, I was bodysurfing. The morning of the Grand Final, I was catching waves in the Indian Ocean. That got me in the perfect headspace.

Then came breakfast – three eggs on multigrain toast with butter every single morning, maybe with bacon on game day for extra fuel. We went for a team walk at West Perth Oval. We threw the frisbee. My hammy felt great. And I got a little nap done, too, just before noon. It's something worth doing during the day before a night game. Just 20 minutes to recharge. Everything was kind of perfect.

I've used the word 'invincible' before, and Paul Roos rightly lit into me, but on the morning of a game – any game – that's when I really do feel invincible, like I'm at my very best. And that's as it should be. You do your preparation to feel as good as you can, come the weekend. You've done your recovery, you've carb-loaded, you're hydrated, you've had good sleep, you've had some anti-inflammatories to fix any soreness. I like to call it Max Day. It's my day. I get to choose what's on TV. I get to choose what time I go for the walk, what time I have my eggs, and it's just a great feeling. You're set, you're ready, and you know that today's the day.

CHAPTER 29

The 2021 AFL Grand Final

Saturday September 25, 5:15pm

Optus Stadium

Melbourne (21.14.140) versus Western Bulldogs (10.6.66)

On the bus to the ground, everyone wears headphones, apart from me – it's just row after row of AirPods and Beats By Dr Dre. Whoever ends up sitting next to me I encourage to take them off and chat, because I really don't want to get into game mode that early. There's no point in listening to 'Lose Yourself' by Eminem three hours before the bounce on a loaded bus. I like to have a laugh and a joke. Sometimes I sit near the coaches for that reason. As you get older, you work out you've got to get closer and closer to the front, with the younger players in the back. I used to be a back-row bandit, but not anymore. It's more efficient to be close to the front anyway. You get into the changerooms first, if you want to get strapped early. And you get into the security line at the airport first – that's a crucial one.

We actually got followed by a chopper on the way to the game, which was a bit funny. It had to be terrible vision, and you wonder who would even be watching us. I think we lost them when we went into a tunnel, a little bit like losing a cop car when you're playing Grand Theft Auto. Honestly, I'm pretty relaxed until maybe twenty minutes before the game, when we start moving a little and doing some tackling, when we're warming up and there's a bit of music on. But even when I'm *on*, I'm still calm, right up to the bounce. Every now and then I chuck in a joke at the coin toss with the umpire. I just like to keep composed in that way.

In the rooms with Goody, we went over our messages again. We had talked about how the Western Bulldogs might set up for us. We had played them three times, and we had noticed them change the way they had played since the Round 19 clash. They used to be a really big switching team, and then they stopped, or at least they switched far less. Sammy Radford, our oppo man, identified that. It meant we needed to watch the likes of Caleb Daniel and Bailey Dale even more. They can really pierce you with their inside passing. You've got to watch out for 'deception kicks' – balls that look like they're kicking *here*, but really they're kicking *there*. Once they're able to bite off those options, they move it inside and get their run going, and before you know it, their ball movement is chaining forward fast.

That's the nuts and bolts, but the coaches also know how to keep the mood light. Goody and Yze had gone missing for a couple of days in quarantine, and it turned out it was because they both had gastro. With that in mind, the media guys had doctored a clip from a movie, I think it was *Dumb and Dumber*, where one of the guys – Jeff Bridges – is having this horrible attack of the runs. Our IT guy had put Goody's face on Bridges' body, which gave everyone a good laugh. Nothing lightens up things quite like bad toilet humour, but we needed those kinds of gags. There was something massive happening on the ground outside, Birds of Tokyo playing all these covers. Stupid jokes kept your mind in here, rather than what was happening out there.

As for inspiring speeches, it's strange – you would think ego would come into it as a coach. You would think 'The Big Grand Final Day Speech' is something they dream about for years, and prepare in their mind over time. But Goody went straight to another coach. He went to Neale Daniher. Neale has been coming in and speaking to our group for years, of course, and he's always inspiring. We have his quotes all over the walls at AAMI Park. Goody hadn't touched on those in a while. Today was the day.

He spoke about the continuum we're all on – on a line between selfish or selfless. ('Nothing great can get done with selfish people, nothing,' Daniher once told us. 'To be great together, you have to be over here – selfless.') But the main one Goody reminded us of was probably my favourite Neale quote: 'When all is said and done, more is said than done. And the mark of a person is not what you say, it's what you do. So, what are you going to do?'

From there, we focused on our warm-ups, and the start. I did everything I needed to do, and even watched a little bit of John Butler. I never get overwhelmed in the moment, but I looked around and people were all up in the stands drinking, partying to the music, and I remember thinking, 'Geez, we're the main event here. This actually might be a bit much.' So I took myself away, went back and sat in the rooms and drank a Red Bull with Harry Petty, and had a bit more fun in there until it was time to go.

The walk out onto the ground was a bit unique. They don't tell you this in advance, but the Fremantle and West Coast players, when they're playing a home game, walk through a bar to get out onto the ground. Sounds bizarre, right? You honestly walk through a bar, and there's people sinking pints and high-fiving you.

Then I got to the oval and there was a little Auskick girl waiting to walk out with me – I didn't know I would have one at the start of the game. 'Are you coming out with me?' I asked, and she goes, 'Yeah. Why not?' I gave her a high five and asked her if she was scared, and told her to watch out for the fireworks. She ran out with me and bolted for the banner – it was the only thing that stopped her leading us onto the field by herself.

I think we also missed a memo about the team photos. They're always taken straight after the banner, but nobody reminded me, and we had to be called back quickly to take the shot. Luckily I'm the captain, so I know exactly where I've gotta be in the frame, but everyone else would have wondered where to stand or sit. The warm-up was a bit rushed as a result, getting only a few kicks and bounces in before we headed into our line for the anthem and the Welcome to Country. And then it starts, and I'm right in the middle.

Everyone's favourite line when we're walking to any first bounce is, 'It starts with you, big fella.' *Yeah mate, I know.* I know I'm going to be the first contest. I know it starts with me. I've known it every game I've rucked since I was a kid. But you say these things anyway, because they feel right. 'You get to do the first contest, mate!' they yell. 'You get to do it!'

And I do love it, although I actually tend to lose a lot more first centre bounces than I win. It's been a development point in my mind for a while, to be a better starter in general. I always have great second halves, but being a better first-quarter player could be more impactful. Darren Burgess knows that. He keeps reminding me. Literally the moment I leave the huddle for the square, he comes up to my ear: 'Throw the first punch.'

The siren blew, and that was the loudest I have ever heard a crowd. But then the umpire waits seven seconds to bounce the ball, so there's this lull before it happens, and everyone goes quiet, and it's nerve-wracking, and before you know it you're flying at the Sherrin. If you have a look at the replay at that ruck contest, it is the clearest free-kick to me I've ever seen in my life. Stefan Martin comes into it really hot, takes his eye off the ball and goes straight over me. Neither of us get the hit-out. But the umpire is never going to ping someone for a rucking free kick to start the Grand Final, so immediately I was thinking, 'Damn, I should have done that!' That was really smart from Stef.

I got a quick, clean handball early, which felt great, but the play was immediately chaotic and harsh. Viney smacks into Macrae. Liberatore smacks into Clayton. It was big early. It was on early. Libba won the clearance and then we had to defend a few inside 50s to start the game.

In the Preliminary Final I had felt really hot and sweaty and nervous at the start. I couldn't breathe properly in the first three minutes. I thought that was going to come again, but it didn't. I didn't feel overwhelmed, either. I had a few contested marks, and a shot on goal, and felt comfortable flying for taps. And we got off to a good start.

Oliver was in everything. Petracca's goal from 50, off one step, while turning a full 180 degrees, was breathtaking. It's hard to imagine putting that much power on the footy with so little time on your pivot foot, but it just *rocketed* through the goals. I think it went 60 metres, carrying the line and smashing into the fence on the full. Viney started really hot as well. And Angus, too. I've talked about how Angus has real inside skills for a wingman – and they came shining right through in the contest. We were up. It was 29 to 8 at quarter-time.

Petracca is one of the best at *not* focusing during on-ground breaks, particularly if something's happening on the big screen. He's a distractible kid. And we happened to be positioned where the Grand Final Sprint was finishing. If Trac gets distracted by 'dancecam' on the big screen, what do you think is going to happen when the Grand Final Sprint – won by Eagles defender Josh Rotham – is ending a few metres away from the midfielders line meeting? That was just another unique moment. They really could have got a better bloody spot to run the 100 metres.

It's unrelated, but we started the second quarter really poorly. Treloar kicked two goals, and Bontempelli kicked two goals, and after that there was a bit of a tie for a little bit throughout the rest of the quarter, with both teams playing some good football.

I threaded a goal from a set shot, and it was called a behind, but it was pure. It was as good as I've kicked a footy in a long time. It could not be more clear – it went to the left side of the post. I was already turning to the crowd with a little finger shaking, but then I've looked at the umpire. I shook my head about that one, and it's interesting to watch back on tape. I honestly didn't realise that I show so much emotion on the ground. In my own head I feel like I just shrugged a little, but later I watched and thought: 'Wow, I must really piss people off by showing that much emotion.' Every time I give away a free kick or something goes against me, you can see it all over my face. 'Geez, just take it on the chin, Max.'

But that actually was a big moment for me, because once it was called a behind, it went straight back down the other end, and Bont took a mark and kicked one of his goals. I could have kicked a captain's goal, but instead he did. I was grumpy. I felt we had let them back in. In truth they forced their way back in. They kicked six goals to one that quarter, and led by eight points at half-time. But I was okay.

I was reset already, but I could also sense a little anger in some of the players, or maybe it was just urgency. There's been some commentary already around that half-time break – that there might have been a weird feeling in our rooms – but I didn't feel that at all. We had that 10 minutes of quietness that we always do. Observers might have just read the wrong message into that moment of reflection.

We worked out our issues, and basically we weren't working hard enough. Sometimes it really is that simple. Treloar's work rate to run up and down, up and down, up and down – and to get those two goals – was better than Trac and Clarry's. But it was also only one quarter. Anyone can get beaten by their man in a quarter. We all wore that on the chin.

Goody is a really composed game-day coach. He tinkered with a couple of things. The Dogs had done a few things differently to what we expected – they had gone back to switching the ball, for instance. 'Boys, they're doing this, so let's change this,' was what he said. 'And work harder.'

It didn't fix everything, of course. The Doggies would have been up and about at half-time, and they took that into the second half. We faced another barrage at the start of the third quarter. I didn't think it would happen like that, where they had 10 inside 50s in five minutes, and back stoppage after back stoppage. I was buggered. My match fitness was a little iffy anyway, having only played two games in a month, and coming off early in both of those. I had really started to feel it, then Bont kicked his third goal, and they were up by 19 points in the premiership quarter.

That was just a massive moment. I'd love to say I was completely composed, and my mind was sticking utterly to the process, but I'm human. I'm a Melbourne supporter. Being 19 points down in a grand final is a completely different story than 44 points down in Round 23. I'm not going to sugarcoat it – everyone was nervous.

But there was one other way of looking at it. We were under siege at that moment. The ball was just stuck in our D50. Our backs were holding up really well, but every time we got it we just couldn't escape. They would intercept or we would cough it up or they would get a free kick and the footy just kept flying back at the Doggies' goals. We had no answer. We needed a reprieve, a fresh start, and oddly enough a goal to them meant we finally got that. We had a centre bounce – a chance to get our game going from there.

That's exactly what we did, in the end. I was in there for the first bounce, and then I came off the ground, and me and Goody had a long chat while watching Luke Jackson and Stef Martin rucking against each other. I said to Goody, 'I think Jacko is jumping over Stef here.' We decided then that I would come back on, take a ruck contest and then push forward, leaving Jacko to ruck out the quarter. He was the perfect match-up.

To be fair, I've watched the clips from that quarter, and Stef's ruck work is great – I think he wins most of the hit-outs. But Jacko's follow-up at ground level was so good. The last one was the most amazing. He just sprints out of the centre like a wingman, gathers low and gives a perfectly weighted handball to Clayton, and I think that's Jacko's only disposal in that whole period, but his presence in there – jumping and bouncing and moving – just felt so important. It created this confusion, and then bang – goals for Bayley, Trac, Ben Brown, Sparrow, Clarry. We went from 19 points down to four goals up going into the last quarter.

At three-quarter time, we spoke a little bit about how we were going, and what the Doggies might do. The message we shared was to play honest footy – to defend the first 10 minutes – and play simply and with strength. I spoke to Trac as well. There was another little distraction for him – a male streaker in jocks, who got smashed by the security guards. It turned out to be the cousin of Peter Bol, the 800-metre runner who finished fourth at the Olympics. Bol even did a post about it later: 'I didn't do all that training with you so you could run onto the bloody ground in a grand final!'

But I just remember looking at Trac, and he was in his head, taking a few deep breaths. Petracca wants to be a big-time player, so I just said, 'Trac, you're made for this. This is your stage.' And to be fair, it was. He had already done his thing. He already had 30 touches and two goals. He's a big, deep thinker, and has great positive self-talk.

He's matured so much over the years. Honestly, before that final quarter began I just thought to myself, 'Wow, what a man you've become.'

We won the centre bounces straight away in the last, so we were actually able to defend from our front half. We were just surging, kicking away quite early. Everyone has their moment – the goal or the contest where they felt we had it won. For me, that was Nibbler's goal.

It was 10 minutes into the last quarter. Stef Martin outmarked me, and kicked it forward, but Hibbo chopped it off. Christian Salem and Trac got involved, and they worked it all the way up the wing together, until it spilled to Ed Langdon, and he popped a little pass over the top. Alex Neal-Bullen took the mark 45 metres out on a slight angle. He went back, kicked truly, and we were up by 42 points with 15 minutes of time left to play. I haven't really watched the last quarter. I've watched the first three quite a lot, so I'm going on memory, and Nibbler is my memory. It was that combination of margin and time. I knew we had won.

I know people were calling at that point to get James Jordon on the field. He had been the medical sub for all three finals, and it would have been great to get him out there. James Harmes was cramping a bit, but that's not a true injury, and our club doctor, Dr Laura Lallenec, wasn't about to play fast and loose. I suppose in hindsight, given the hamstring tear Steven May was carrying, we could have subbed him off. But you're not thinking in those terms.

You're playing out the most important game of the year. It's hard to switch off the focus required to be out there on that stage. I played the game out with hardly a smile. It's the way I've been drilled. For instance, the Dogs defender Taylor Duryea went off late in the game, and during that pause Trac was telling everyone to smile. And I was getting angry: 'Trac, I don't want to smile. I need to get down the line here or Stef might get a mark.' But really, Trac was right, and I needed to snap out of it.

I remember an effort from Clayton Oliver with three minutes to go. Bontempelli took a mark that I thought Clayton could have spoiled. And I think Jake Lever had a go: 'Come on, Clayton, spoil that!' I was going to say something as well, and then I looked at Clayton, and he's got that big grin on his face, and we're up by 70, and I switched gears and started grinning, too: 'No, that's allright. That's fine, Clayton. You do you, mate.'

I've never been in a situation where there's no next week and you're happy about that fact, so it was a weird feeling. I was happy, but I wasn't ecstatic until that final siren went. That's when I could see that the drought was done. Tom McDonald had his shot at goal after the siren. I probably would have torped the ball into the crowd, or taken the Sherrin in hand and started running the other way, doing a lap of honour with the footy in hand. I definitely wouldn't have taken the set shot, because I would have missed it anyway, which would have been an anticlimax. Tommy drilled it home, for a 74-point win.

On the siren itself, I was with Ed Langdon, who'd become a really close friend in the past year, with the hub only escalating that. It was great that we were side by side in that moment. I got over to Tommy first, when he kicked his goal, and then I was flooded by people and players.

I remember I made sure I was going to shake hands with Bontempelli, and I was lucky he was close to me, so it worked out quite well. But I was always going to find him as soon as I could. I'm a tremendous fan of his and what he does leadership-wise, and as a person. I also just think it's a good gesture to show the other team some sympathy and true respect before you go and celebrate yourself, because the Grand Final is a very in-your-face celebration, with the other team required to stay on the ground. Bont had an amazing year, and so did the Dogs, and I wanted to let him know that.

I probably still hadn't taken the moment in until Abbey Holmes got to me. Normally when I'm on TV, I don't think about how many people are watching, but right then I did. And I realised that this interview would be watched by every Melbourne supporter, and I made sure I said what I knew they were all thinking, and what I was thinking as well.

I'm a Melbourne fan. And ours is a club that's been followed by tragedy, with the passing of Dean Bailey, Colin Sylvia, Troy Broadbridge, Robbie Flower, Sean Wight, Jim Stynes – and of course Neale Daniher is still fighting his battle. I wanted to mention those guys, and I unfortunately missed a couple of names, but I basically wanted everyone to know that the Demons are who we are because of those people. I made sure I recognised the eastern states, too, remembering how tough they were doing it back home. And as soon as I said that, I knew that we had done something for a good reason, with a greater meaning.

After that, it's just one by one picking people off that you have to congratulate. There's so many people on the ground – almost 75 in the hub plus a couple of other key people, board members and what not who've made their way onto the grass. The stage got set up so quickly, and then I started to get worked up about my speech. I knew I had to thank our sponsors, so our media manager drew up a little dot point list ready to go, and I nailed them, and repeated what I had told Abbey, and then just stood back with everyone else listening to Basil Zempilas.

Trac already knew that he was the Norm Smith medallist. I think someone must have told him to stand closer to the front. It was probably obvious that he was best on ground, but I still feel like that somewhat ruined the surprise for Trac. There's a funny bit of vision when you watch it back – he walks toward the stage before his name even gets called. He's literally on the move before he even hears 'Christian Petracca'.

And then one by one, everyone gets a medal. I forgot that the captain gets skipped, so that he can come back on stage with the coach. It meant I was the last one up. My little Auskick girl was back and she goes, 'Congratulations, you finally did it. Well done on breaking our drought', and I remember laughing inside thinking, 'You're six – it hasn't been that hard for you.'

Goody was supposed to make a speech but that didn't happen, and that was a real shame, because we had divided up who to thank or speak about, and one of us was going to mention Nathan Jones, and we thought Goody was probably the best one to do it. He never got that chance, so we missed a pretty key moment to thank a pretty key pillar – one of our greatest heroes in the changing of the guard. But I'm sure he knows how much he means to us.

And then you've got to stare at a camera for minutes on end, holding this screaming-with-joy pose, pretending that you're yelling, but you're not really yelling, so that all the photographers can get their shots.

When that was done, Hibbo decided to run off with the cup. He's always the life of the party, and he was very good in the celebrations from that moment onwards. It really got into Michael Hibberd areas as soon as that siren went. He just tore away with it, and got all the way to the crowd before we realised he wasn't coming back and we had to get over there with him. Hibbo was one of the very lucky ones, in that he had some family members that don't live in Victoria or New South Wales and were able to come to the game. He must have known where they were, because he ran straight to them.

That part of the day was one of the more surreal parts for me. I've always dreamed of winning a grand final, and in that dream it's always daytime, it's always at the MCG, and that lap of honour is one of those moments where you're supposed to run into all these people you know. Your schoolmates. A couple of workmates. Former teammates. Old sponsors. Family. Extended family. You keep bumping into people on that one amazing lap. The Perth crowd was phenomenal, but I knew nobody.

From there, we all sort of grouped up. The Western Australian boys – Luke Jackson, Nev Jetta, Kozzy Pickett – had family to see, so we waited while they lingered and hugged, but soon we were into the rooms. I was the first one inside, so instead of there being a mass of people waiting and cheering, it was quiet, and then it started to build, and then we belted out that song. The day I don't sing the song with total gusto is the day I retire, and we gave it the full shake. Bernie Vince was singing with us, which is hilarious given he's been retired and a commentator for three years now. I dashed off after that to find my phone, and FaceTime home. Calling Jess. Then Mum and Dad. Then my brother. I came back out and did some TV, but the changerooms wasn't my vibe. There was so much media, so many conversations. I headed out onto the ground, where Angus Brayshaw and Ed Langdon had a couple of cigars. Someone bought a little speaker and we started playing music. One of the songs was 'Freed from Desire'. I heard later that the Bulldogs had sung that song in their changerooms after their Preliminary Final win, and it had made it onto the AFL Instagram account, so there was this idea that we co-opted their song and might have been taunting or trolling them, but that's not it at all. It's just a cracker of a song.

This might surprise some people, but I still wasn't feeling that exact feeling I craved after winning a flag. There was something missing from the experience. It arrived moments later. We went back down into the rooms, and then into the smaller changeroom part of the complex, where you get showered and dressed and ready, and someone put the speaker on in there, and before you knew it all 75 people from our hub were crammed in there, and we just started *belting* out these tunes.

We would have gone through about 20 songs, all of them bangers like 'Sweet Caroline' by Neil Diamond and 'Take Me Home, Country Roads' by John Denver. It just turned into this hour-long sing-a-long with beer and champagne, and we knew that with players retiring or staff departing it would be the only time we would all be in a room together like that again – that it was a moment in time.

No-one was watching and yet everyone was watching, and we just got to be a group and let our hair down and let loose. That's easily my favourite memory from the day. I would have been happy to catch the redeye flight home that night. We had our one amazing hour after a long amazing season.

CHAPTER 30

Aftermath

I forgot to shower. I can't believe it, but I forgot to shower. Most of the guys found a moment early on in the rooms to have a rinse and get changed, but not all of us. There were five or six of us in the same boat, or rather, the same bus. We all had to get onboard to get to the venue for the night, in the Market Grounds of Perth. That was that, so all of a sudden I'm on a bus wearing my dirty boots, socks, shorts and jumper. I sat with Tommy McDonald and we FaceTimed Lynden Dunn. We tried a few other people and they didn't pick up. Imagine that, the premiership captain FaceTimes from the bus after the game, and you screen the call.

We got to the venue and there was this massive, snaking line of 500 people, and we go straight to the front, ushered into our own area, and at that point you start feeling like

LeBron James and the Lakers. We had our own little private area. That's where the footage of me on Adam Tomlinson's shoulders emerged. I was actually sitting in the back corner talking to a few older people there – I'm more of a talker than a dancer. Then at some point I thought I'll go see Tommo and say hello. I ended up on his shoulders, the video went viral, and suddenly I was 'best on' for the afterparty.

We finished up at about 4 am that night, and got on the bus back to Joondalup Resort. The only tricky part was, they're quite a busy resort, and they were completely booked the next day. So we had to check out at 9 am. Imagine it. We've been there almost five weeks. There's a lot of stuff strewn about our rooms. We got back from celebrating the 2021 AFL Premiership some time after 4 am, and had a few hours to get some sleep, get packed, and get back on a bus. That was a hard, hard check-out.

We headed to Forrest Place in Perth's CBD to do a meet and greet, and show our faces to the faithful. I got an amazing buzz out of that. If we had been in Melbourne, yes, Yarra Park would have been busting with 25,000 Demons fans or more, and by comparison there might have been 5000 Melbourne supporters turn out in Perth, but they filled the place, and they were desperate to celebrate. I loved being able to give something back.

We had a full day at the Cottesloe Hotel, too. We had a courtyard out back to ourselves, which we didn't leave all day. Family and friends and everyone from the hub started rocking up, and by 4 pm the place was packed. The Melbourne theme song was getting a good run with the DJ, and soon enough I had Goody sitting up on my shoulders, and that went viral, too.

The next few days, we stayed at the Mercure, and there were other things to do, like signing day – sitting for an entire day signing every piece of premiership merchandise and memorabilia you can imagine. There were exit meetings, too, which are important for not only improvement but also to give the people who might be leaving some clarity and closure.

I tried to take one for the team, by asking the leadership to make my meeting early in the day. I didn't want to stitch up one of the young guys who'd been out partying by asking them to turn up for an exit interview at 9 am. Let them have their sleep. My meeting was strange though, because, really, what can you say? I was in there with the coaches and footy manager, and honestly, we all just started clapping. It made sense in the moment, because even if my year wasn't overly successful personally, what we did together was enough. And the people in that room were just as much a part of it all, so we all just clapped one another.

We did talk about what I want to get out of next year, and what I've found in my football. That seemed clear to me – I liked what I had learned off Jacko, and feel like the next step for me is being more dangerous after the rucking contest, involving myself as a stoppage threat, or even more as a forward. There's elements of my game I need to work on as much as anyone.

Eight of us finally left Perth on the Thursday, keen to get home. I took the cup with me, and had it to myself in Melbourne that weekend. Coming back in the door to see Jess, with the premiership cup in hand and a medal around my neck, was a great way to make an appearance.

The next day, I made sure to get a viewing for Don McLardy, our former president. I arranged for his son to get him down to a park in Sorrento, just him, a private affair. I think he thought his son was going to propose to his girlfriend, so he got all dressed up. Then I rocked up with the cup. He was thrilled – *like he had played the game himself* – and I was thrilled for him. He was at the helm during that unfortunate 2011–2012 period, and deserved more for his efforts, because he lives and breathes Melbourne.

Then I settled back into life in Melbourne a little, and that was beautiful. Things were still locked down, but perversely – because the season was over – I felt like I had all this freedom. Suddenly I didn't have strict AFL restrictions looming over everything I did or everywhere I went. I was able to do whatever the general public was doing. I could go to Coles and get food for the house. I could walk down the street and get a coffee. I could go to the beach.

I'm presuming I'll be fitter than ever when the pre-season really kicks into gear, because we can't really travel much yet, and I reckon I've had the least amount of alcohol in any season I've played. I'm not a big drinker anyway, but I've already started running again – that thing I once hated but now love.

It's hard to say what's driving me into 2022. People want us to say that we're driven to win next year so that the fans locked down at home this season can see it all in person, and that's absolutely true, but I also stop to think about how *hard* it is to win a premiership – how you need everything to go right, and how it's not just going to happen for us. I think it's a realistic goal for us, and it's where we should set our sights, but winning it again would be a bonus.

The players who missed out this season will be part of that driving force. They'll be keen to set extremely high pre-season standards. We will need to improve. If we stay the same, we won't win again, because the competition moves on quickly. There's a very good reason that no premiership side has ever taken to the field together again.

But I think Goody will figure out how to address us going forward. Last pre-season, he and I had some long and robust summer discussions about what we wanted to achieve, how we would set it up, and the language we were going to use. Goody will make sure he gets that language right again, and set those goals out from the very beginning. I suspect his focus will revolve around family and friends, and connection. Connection is important to him, because it's what football clubs are about. That's their heart, beating true.

Last year we had a great idea. We wanted to add something to our Saturday morning hill sessions – an hour of pretty intense hill running. Sprint up and jog down, sprint up and jog down. What we came up with was using those sessions as a chance to invite past players along. I asked David Neitz about it one day, to see how many of the old group wanted to come down. He wasn't sure, but suspected quite a few.

I turned up and there were 50 blokes.

They ran up with us, and because they're a bit older they slowed it down for us, which was nice. But it became a cultural event rather than just a fitness event. To get down there and see James Strauss and Tom Couch and Anthony Ingerson was such a brilliant thing. They all came to lunch afterwards, too, at Hobba in Prahran. We just squeezed everybody in – nearly 100 people all up. We wanted to keep those sessions going, but COVID got in the way. We thought about doing similar sessions with partners and girlfriends, too, and hopefully we will.

It's important to me because part of the reason we play football is the sense of community we can create, and the impact we can have – the way we can make Melbourne supporters proud, and how we can make those people who know us feel proud of us, and close to us. That's the bigger reason we play, according to Goody. He has a phrase for it: the higher purpose.

The higher purpose is James Harmes being best mates with John, the boy with Down syndrome. Or it's Jake Lever heading to the Royal Children's Hospital because he's found a connection with a sick kid called Noah. Majak Daw – after what he's been through – is playing for a higher purpose. Kysaiah Pickett – with his early struggles in life – is playing for a higher purpose. I think of the whole team and the reason they all play, and the supporters and the reasons they all watch, and I think there's a higher purpose at the heart of it all.

I've never seen a group connect with their fans like Melbourne do, and perhaps that's because we've been there with them in some of the darkest days, and they've been with us. It really feels like we have something in common – a shared experience of grief and then joy. Playing the game now that the drought is broken feels like it's about pride, and love, and proving that what we have in this moment isn't some flash in the pan but something real. Something true. Something pure.

MELBOURNE'S 2021 SEASON SUMMARY

Club	Q1	Q2	Q3	Q4	Score	Margin	Result	Ground	Date	Ladder result
Round 1										
Melbourne	4.4	7.6	9.8	11.14	80	22	WON	MCG	20 March	3rd
Fremantle	0.4	3.8	6.9	8.10	58					
Round 2										
St. Kilda	3.2	6.3	8.4	11.7	73					
Melbourne	3.4	6.7	9.13	12.19	91	18	WON	Marvel Stadium	27 Mar	4th
Round 3										
GWS	5.1	7.1	8.1	11.2	68					
Melbourne	2.3	6.5	10.7	15.12	102	34	WON	Manuka Oval	4 April	3rd
Round 4										
Melbourne	2.4	6.8	9.9	12.13	85	25	WON	MCG	11 April	2nd
Geelong	1.1	3.3	8.3	9.6	60					
Round 5										
Hawthorn	4.3	5.3	6.6	8.6	54					
Melbourne	2.5	4.7	7.10	15.14	104	50	WON	MCG	18 April	2nd
Round 6										
Melbourne	2.2	6.6	10.8	12.10	82	34	WON	MCG	24 April	2nd
Richmond	3.3	3.7	5.8	6.12	48					
Round 7										
North Melbourne	4.1	9.5	10.6	11.7	73	30	WON	Blundstone Arena	2 May	1st
Melbourne	3.2	6.4	12.7	16.7	103					
Round 8										
Melbourne	3.1	5.6	8.6	10.7	67	9	WON	MCG	8 May	1st
Sydney	3.3	3.7	6.8	8.10	58					

Club	Q1	Q2	Q3	Q4	Score	Margin	Result	Ground	Date	Ladder result
Round 9										
Melbourne	4.3	8.6	12.9	13.16	94	26	WON	MCG	16 May	1st
Carlton	3.2	6.5	8.7	10.8	68					
Round 10										
Adelaide	4.2	8.4	11.5	15.6	96	1				
Melbourne	5.1	8.4	11.8	14.11	95		lost	Adelaide Oval	22 May	2nd
Round 11										
Western Bulldogs	2.2	6.5	6.8	8.11	59					
Melbourne	6.5	9.6	12.8	13.9	87	28	WON	Marvel Stadium	28 May	1st
Round 12										
Melbourne	2.3	5.4	10.9	14.13	97	22	WON	Giants Stadium	4 June	1st
Brisbane Lions	4.4	8.6	10.8	11.9	75					
Round 13										
Melbourne	2.2	4.4	8.6	9.9	63		LOST	SCG	14 June	1st
Collingwood	1.4	6.8	8.11	11.14	80	17				
Round 14 bye										
Melbourne										1st
Round 15										
Essendon	2.3	4.5	6.7	8.9	57					
Melbourne	1.5	4.8	8.12	9.14	68	11	WON	MCG	26 June	1st
Round 16										
Melbourne	1.3	3.6	5.9	7.13	55		LOST	MCG	3 July	2nd
GWS	2.2	6.6	8.8	9.10	64	9				
Round 17										
Port Adelaide	2.2	5.3	7.5	8.7	55					
Melbourne	3.2	8.4	10.9	12.14	86	31	WON	Adelaide Oval	8 July	1st
Round 18										
Melbourne	4.4	6.7	9.10	11.13	79	0	DRAW	MCG	17 July	1st
Hawthorn	1.2	5.2	10.3	12.7	79					

MELBOURNE'S 2021 SEASON SUMMARY

Club	Q1	Q2	Q3	Q4	Score	Margin	Result	Ground	Date	Ladder result
Round 19										
Melbourne	1.4	2.7	7.9	9.11	65		LOST	MCG	24 July	3rd
Western Bulldogs	3.2	6.4	10.5	13.7	85	20				
Round 20										
Gold Coast	3.2	3.3	3.3	4.6	30					
Melbourne	6.4	12.8	17.14	18.20	128	98	WON	Marvel Stadium	1 August	3rd
Round 21										
West Coast	2.0	4.5	5.6	9.9	63					
Melbourne	4.2	5.3	10.8	10.12	72	9	WON	Optus Stadium	9 August	1st
Round 22										
Melbourne	3.3	7.4	12.7	16.8	104	41	WON	MCG	15 August	1st
Adelaide	1.6	3.7	8.8	9.9	63					
Round 23										
Geelong	2.1	10.2	12.3	12.5	77					
Melbourne	2.3	3.5	6.7	12.9	81	4	WON	GMHBA Stadium	21 August	1st
First Qualifying Final										
Melbourne	5.4	9.10	9.12	13.15	93	33	WON	Adelaide Oval	28 August	
Brisbane Lions	4.2	5.4	7.5	9.6	60					
First Preliminary Final										
Melbourne	5.3	9.6	17.8	19.11	125	83	WON	Optus Stadium	10 September	
Geelong	1.0	5.1	5.2	6.6	42					
Grand Final										
Melbourne	4.5	5.9	12.11	21.14	140	74	WON	Optus Stadium	25 September	
Western Bulldogs	1.2	7.5	9.5	10.6	66					

ACKNOWLEDGEMENTS

My thanks to my family.

Thanks to my manager.

Thanks to all my teammates, past and present.

Thanks to the Melbourne Football Club and all the staff and people who make it a great club, past and present.

Thanks to Melbourne's past players and legends.

Thanks to the AFL.

And lastly thanks to the Melbourne fans ...

PICTURE CREDITS

The publisher would like to thank AFL Photos and their photographers.

Front cover Max Gawn: Michael Willson
Front cover background: Quinn Rooney

Section 1: Page 1 Dylan Burns (top and bottom), page 2 Mark Metcalfe (top) Quinn Rooney (bottom), Page 3 Michael Willson (top) Dylan Burns (bottom left and right), Page 4 Robert Cianflone (top) Michael Willson (bottom), Page 5 Quinn Rooney (top) Sarah Reed (bottom), Page 6 Quinn Rooney (top) Cameron Spencer (bottom), Page 7 Matt King (top) Michael Willson (middle) Daniel Pockett (bottom), Page 8 Dylan Burns (top) James Elsby (bottom).

Section 2: Page 1 Daniel Pockett (top) Quinn Rooney (bottom), Page 2 Michael Willson (top) Daniel Carson (bottom), Page 3 Quinn Rooney (top) Daniel Pockett (bottom), Page 4 Sarah Reed (top and bottom), Page 5 Will Russell (top) Paul Kane (bottom), Page 6 Michael Willson (top) Paul Kane (middle left and right) Paul Kane (bottom), Page 7 Gary Day (top) Michael Willson (middle) Daniel Carson (bottom), Page 8 Dylan Burns (top left) Daniel Carson (top right) Will Russell (middle) Michael Willson (bottom).